PROOFREADING, REVISING, & EDITING SKILLS SUCCESS
IN 20 MINUTES A DAY

PROOFREADING, REVISING, & EDITING SKILLS SUCCESS

IN 20 MINUTES A DAY

Brady Smith

LEARNINGEXPRESS®

NEW YORK

Library of Congress Cataloging-in-Publication Data:
Smith, Brady.
  Proofreading, revising, and editing skills : success in 20 minutes a day /
Brady Smith.—1st ed.
    p. cm.
  ISBN 1-57685-466-3
  1. Report writing—Handbooks, manuals, etc. 2. Proofreading—Handbooks,
manuals, etc. 3. Editing—Handbooks, manuals, etc. I. Title.
  LB1047.3.S55 2003
  808'.02—dc21   2002013959

Printed in the United States of America
9 8 7 6 5 4 3 2 1
First Edition

ISBN 1-57685-466-3

For more information or to place an order, contact LearningExpress at:
    55 Broadway
    8th Floor
    New York, NY 10006

Or visit us at:
    www.learnatest.com

About the Author

Brady Smith teaches English at Adlai E. Stevenson High School in the Bronx, New York. His work has been previously published in textbooks, and this is his first complete book. He would like to dedicate this book to Julie, Gillian, and Isabel, with love.

Contents

▶ How to Use This Book

Since you are reading this right now, let us assume you have at least one draft of your writing that you want to proofread, revise, and edit in order to present a well-written and clear finished piece. As all good writers know, a first draft needs to be cleaned up, trimmed down, and organized. This book is designed to help you do just that—in 20 short lessons in just 20 minutes a day.

This book stands alone as a teaching tool. You can pick it up and learn a new skill at any point during the writing process. Whether you are prewriting, drafting, editing, revising, or working on a final copy, this book will become a useful reference guide. You may find it helpful to turn to this book as you finish different sections of your writing because it can help you correct as you write. Or you can read the lessons in this book and then go back to your own piece of writing—just to reinforce important writing skills. No matter which method you choose, you will accomplish what you set out to do: master the skills you need to proofread, revise, and edit your writing.

Proofreading, Revising, and Editing Skills Success in 20 Minutes a Day begins with a discussion about the steps to create a piece of writing, and then gives you the coaching you will need to correct any errors you find in your work. It walks you through the revision process by showing you how to transform your sentences from awkward and choppy sentence fragments and run-ons to clear, concise expressions. It shows you how to organize paragraphs and how to use transitions skillfully. You will also learn the fundamental rules of noun/pronoun agreement as well as subject/verb agreement. When you are finished with this book, you will find that your writing has improved, has style and detail, and is free of cluttered sentences and common errors.

Some writers think that once a word has been written, it is sacred. Successful writers know that change is an important part of the writing process. Early drafts that may seem finished can most likely be improved. Since writing is a process, you have to be willing to change, rearrange, and discard material to achieve a well-crafted final product. Very few writers create the perfect draft on the first try. Most writers will tell you that writing the first draft is only the beginning and that the majority of the work comes after the initial drafting process. You need to look very closely at your writing, examine it sentence by sentence, and fine-tune it to produce excellence.

Your writing is a reflection of you. The proofreading, revising, and editing processes provide a mirror in which you can examine your writing. Before your writing goes public, you must iron out the transitions between ideas and make sure your paragraphs are structured correctly. You need to clean up your writing and pick out the unnecessary auxiliary verbs from your sentences, perfect your tone, and polish your verbs. Your efforts will show.

Even if you are not currently working on a piece of writing that you need to hand in, present to an audience, or send to a client, this book will teach you the skills that will improve your everyday writing. Each skill outlined in this book is an important part of a good writer's "toolbox." While you will not use every tool for each piece of writing, you will have them ready when you need to apply them.

If you are job hunting, perhaps you need to revise a draft of a cover letter.. This piece of writing is the first impression your employer will have of you, so it's important to submit your best effort. Perhaps you are working on an essay for school. Your teacher's assessment of your abilities will certainly improve if you turn in a composition that shows thoughtful revision, attention to detail, and an understanding of grammatical rules.

Like your ideal final draft, *Proofreading, Revising, and Editing Skills Success in 20 Minutes a Day* has no filler or fluff. It is a book for people who want to learn the editorial skills needed to revise a piece of writing without doing a lot of busy work. Each lesson introduces a skill or concept and offers exercises to practice what you have learned.

Though each lesson is designed to be completed in about 20 minutes, the pace at which you approach the lessons is up to you. After each lesson, you may want to stop and revise your own writing, or you may want to read several lessons in one sitting and then revise your work. No matter how you use this book, you can be sure that your final drafts will improve. Start by taking the pretest to see what you already know and what you need to learn about proofreading, revising, and editing. After you have completed the lessons, you can take the post-test to see how much you have learned. In the appendices, you will find a list of proofreading marks to use as you write, as well as a list of additional resources if you find you need a little extra help.

If you apply what you have learned in this book, you will find that your writing gets positive attention. Teachers, employers, friends, and relatives will all notice your improvement. It is certain, though, that *you* will be the most satisfied of all.

PROOFREADING, REVISING, & EDITING SKILLS SUCCESS
IN 20 MINUTES A DAY

▶ Pretest

Before you begin the lessons in this book, it is a good idea to see how much you already know about proofreading, revising, and editing *and* what you need to learn. This pretest is designed to ask you some basic questions so you can evaluate your needs. Knowing your own strengths and weaknesses can help you focus on the skills that need improvement.

The questions in this pretest do not cover all the topics discussed in each lesson, so even if you can answer every single question in this pretest correctly, there are still many strategies you can learn in order to master the finer points of grammar and style. On the other hand, if there are many questions on the pretest that puzzle you, or if you find that you do not get a good percentage of answers correct, don't worry. This book is designed to take you through the entire proofreading, editing, and revising process, step-by-step.

Each lesson is designed to take 20 minutes, although those of you who score well on the pretest might move more quickly. If your score is lower than you would like it to be, you may want to devote a little more than 20 minutes of practice each day so that you can enhance your skills. Whatever the case, continue with these lessons daily to keep the concepts fresh in your mind, and then apply them to your writing.

An answer sheet is provided for you at the beginning of the pretest. You may mark your answers there, or, if you prefer, circle the correct answer right in the book. If you do not own this book, number a sheet of paper from 1–50 and write your answers there. This is not a timed test. Take as much time as you need, and do your best. Once you have finished, check your answers with the answer key at the end of this test. Every answer includes a reference to a corre-sponding lesson. If you answer a question incor-rectly, turn to the chapter that covers that particu-lar topic, read the information, and then try to answer the question according to the instruction given in that chapter.

Pretest

1.	ⓐ	ⓑ	ⓒ	ⓓ		21.	ⓐ	ⓑ	ⓒ	ⓓ		41.	ⓐ	ⓑ	ⓒ	ⓓ
2.	ⓐ	ⓑ	ⓒ	ⓓ		22.	ⓐ	ⓑ				42.	ⓐ	ⓑ	ⓒ	ⓓ
3.	ⓐ	ⓑ	ⓒ	ⓓ		23.	ⓐ	ⓑ				43.	ⓐ	ⓑ	ⓒ	ⓓ
4.	ⓐ	ⓑ	ⓒ	ⓓ		24.	ⓐ	ⓑ				44.	ⓐ	ⓑ	ⓒ	ⓓ
5.	ⓐ	ⓑ	ⓒ	ⓓ		25.	ⓐ	ⓑ				45.	ⓐ	ⓑ	ⓒ	ⓓ
6.	ⓐ	ⓑ	ⓒ	ⓓ		26.	ⓐ	ⓑ				46.	ⓐ	ⓑ	ⓒ	ⓓ
7.	ⓐ	ⓑ	ⓒ	ⓓ		27.	ⓐ	ⓑ				47.	ⓐ	ⓑ	ⓒ	ⓓ
8.	ⓐ	ⓑ	ⓒ	ⓓ		28.	ⓐ	ⓑ				48.	ⓐ	ⓑ	ⓒ	ⓓ
9.	ⓐ	ⓑ	ⓒ	ⓓ		29.	ⓐ	ⓑ				49.	ⓐ	ⓑ	ⓒ	ⓓ
10.	ⓐ	ⓑ	ⓒ	ⓓ		30.	ⓐ	ⓑ				50.	ⓐ	ⓑ	ⓒ	ⓓ
11.	ⓐ	ⓑ	ⓒ	ⓓ		31.	ⓐ	ⓑ								
12.	ⓐ	ⓑ	ⓒ	ⓓ		32.	ⓐ	ⓑ								
13.	ⓐ	ⓑ	ⓒ	ⓓ		33.	ⓐ	ⓑ								
14.	ⓐ	ⓑ	ⓒ	ⓓ		34.	ⓐ	ⓑ	ⓒ	ⓓ						
15.	ⓐ	ⓑ				35.	ⓐ	ⓑ	ⓒ	ⓓ						
16.	ⓐ	ⓑ	ⓒ	ⓓ		36.	ⓐ	ⓑ	ⓒ	ⓓ						
17.	ⓐ	ⓑ				37.	ⓐ	ⓑ	ⓒ	ⓓ						
18.	ⓐ	ⓑ	ⓒ	ⓓ		38.	ⓐ	ⓑ								
19.	ⓐ	ⓑ	ⓒ	ⓓ		39.	ⓐ	ⓑ	ⓒ	ⓓ						
20.	ⓐ	ⓑ	ⓒ	ⓓ		40.	ⓐ	ⓑ	ⓒ	ⓓ						

1. Which of the following is a complete sentence?
   a. Because night fell.
   b. Jim ate the sandwich.
   c. On a tree-lined path.
   d. In our neck of the woods.

2. Which of the following sentences is correctly punctuated?
   a. In the dead of night. The van pulled up.
   b. Chuck would not, give Jaime the seat.
   c. Over coffee and toast, Kelly told me about her new job.
   d. Lemonade. My favorite drink.

3. Which of the following sentences correctly uses a conjunction?
   a. I cannot play in the game until I practice more.
   b. I hid in the basement my brother was mad at me.
   c. Victor erased the answering machine message Nora would not find out.
   d. She scored a goal won the game.

4. Which of the underlined words or phrases in the following sentence could be deleted without changing the meaning?
   Various <u>different</u> companies offer <u>incentive plans</u> to their <u>employees</u>.
   a. different
   b. incentive
   c. plans
   d. employees

5. Which of the underlined words in the following sentence is an unnecessary qualifier or intensifier?
   Many <u>experts</u> consider the <u>stained</u> glass in <u>that</u> church to be the <u>very</u> best.
   a. experts
   b. stained
   c. that
   d. very

6. Determine whether the italicized phrase in the following sentence is a participial phrase, a gerund phrase, an infinitive phrase, or an appositive phrase.
   Having missed the bus, Allen knew he would be late for work.
   a. participial phrase
   b. gerund phrase
   c. infinitive phrase
   d. appositive phrase

7. Choose the best conjunction to combine this sentence pair.
   We can ask directions. We can use a map.
   a. and
   b. but
   c. or
   d. because

8. The following sentence pair can be revised into one better sentence. Choose the sentence that is the best revision.
   The bicycle tire is flat. The bicycle tire is on the bike.
   a. The bicycle tire is on the bike and the bicycle tire is flat.
   b. The flat bicycle tire is on the bike.
   c. On the bike, the bicycle tire there is flat.
   d. The bicycle tire on the bike is flat.

9. Choose the sentence that begins with a phrase modifier.
 a. He kept his bottle cap collection in a shoebox.
 b. In the event of an emergency, do not panic.
 c. I was pleased to see that my coworker had been promoted.
 d. The octopus has been at the zoo for 20 years.

10. Select the letter for the topic sentence in the following paragraph.
 a. He was born in 1818. **b.** He was educated in the universities of Moscow and St. Petersburg. **c.** In 1852, he abandoned poetry and drama and devoted himself to fiction. **d.** Ivan Turgenev was a critically acclaimed Russian author.

11. Identify the type of organizational structure used in the following paragraph: chronological order, order of importance, spatial order, or order of familiarity.

When you enter the mansion, the great hall has three ornate doorways and a grand staircase. The doorway to the left leads to the kitchen area, the doorway to the right leads to the library, and the doorway straight ahead leads to the formal dining room. The staircase curves up to the second floor. Directly above you will see the famous "Chandelier de Grouton," with over 4,000 crystals shaped like teardrops.
 a. chronological order
 b. order of importance
 c. spatial order
 d. order of familiarity

12. Which of the underlined words in the following sentence is considered transitional?
 We <u>did not</u> catch <u>any</u> fish; <u>as a result</u>, we ate macaroni <u>and</u> cheese.
 a. did not
 b. any
 c. as a result
 d. and

13. Which of the underlined words in the following paragraph is a transition word?

A National Park Service employee <u>annually</u> inspects the famous Mount Rushmore National Memorial <u>near</u> Keystone, South Dakota. He uses ropes and harnesses to take a close look at the 60-foot granite heads of George Washington, Theodore Roosevelt, Thomas Jefferson, <u>and</u> Abraham Lincoln. If he finds a crack, he coats it with a sealant, <u>thereby</u> preventing moisture from cracking it further.
 a. annually
 b. near
 c. and
 d. thereby

14. Identify the purpose of a composition with the following title:
 "Good Reasons to Always Drive Safely"
 a. persuasive
 b. expository
 c. narrative
 d. descriptive

15. Identify whether the following sentence is fact or opinion.
 The voting age should be raised to 21.
 a. fact
 b. opinion

16. Which of the following sentences does *NOT* use informal language?
   a. Everybody said his new car was a "sweet ride."
   b. Susanne totally couldn't believe that she had won the lottery.
   c. The letter arrived in the morning, and he opened it immediately.
   d. I always feel cooped up in my cubicle at work.

17. Identify the appropriate type of language to use in a letter requesting information from a government agency.
   a. formal
   b. informal

18. Which of the following sentences uses the active voice?
   a. Peter was given a laptop to use when he worked at home.
   b. The mountain was climbed by several of the bravest hikers in the group.
   c. The favors for the birthday party were provided by the restaurant.
   d. Randy and Thien won the egg toss at the state fair.

19. Which of the following sentences uses the active voice?
   a. Several ingredients were used by the chef to make the stew.
   b. The chef used several ingredients to make the stew.
   b. To make the stew, several ingredients were used.
   b. The stew was made by the chef using several ingredients.

20. Which of the following sentences does NOT use passive voice?
   a. She is known by the whole town as the best goalie on the hockey team.
   b. The puck was hurled across the ice by the star forward.
   c. She won the Best Player Award last winter.
   d. The women's ice hockey team was founded five years ago.

21. Identify the correct verb for the blank in the following sentence.
   Laura and her friend _____ for their trip to Peru in an hour.
   a. leaves
   b. leave

22. Identify the correct contraction for the blank in the following sentence.
   _____ Jake and Mariela have to work tonight?
   a. Don't
   b. Doesn't

23. Identify the correct verb for the blank in the following sentence.
   We, the entire student body, including one student who graduated mid-year, _____ the school colors to remain green and black.
   a. wants
   b. want

24. Identify the correct verb for the blank in the following sentence.
   A committee _____ policy in all matters of evaluation.
   a. determines
   b. determine

25. Identify the correct verb for the blank in the following sentence.

Neither the bus driver nor the passengers _____ the new route.

a. likes
b. like

26. Identify the correct pronoun(s) for the blank in the following sentence.

Anybody can learn to make _____ own web site.

a. his or her
b. their

27. Identify the correct pronoun for the blank in the following sentence.

I often think of Andra and _____.

a. she
b. her

28. Identify the correct pronoun for the blank in the following sentence.

My brother and _____ used to play ping-pong together every day.

a. I
b. me

29. Identify the correct word for the blank in the following sentence.

Tirso made the basket _____.

a. easy
b. easily

30. Identify the correct word for the blank in the following sentence.

His black eye looked _____.

a. bad
b. badly

31. Identify the correct word for the blank in the following sentence.

The boy told his teacher that he did not perform _____ in the concert because he was sick.

a. good
b. well

32. Identify the correct word for the blank in the following sentence.

That was a _____ good milkshake.

a. real
b. really

33. Identify the correct word for the blank in the following sentence.

Of the three sweaters, I like the red one _____.

a. better
b. best

34. Identify the sentence that uses capitalization correctly.

a. In the movie, David had a difficult time in cuba.
b. in the movie, David had a difficult time in Cuba.
c. In the Movie, David had a difficult time in Cuba.
d. In the movie, David had a difficult time in Cuba.

35. Identify the sentence that uses capitalization correctly.

a. The whole family appreciated the letter Senator Clinton sent to Uncle Jeff.
b. The whole Family appreciated the letter senator Clinton sent to Uncle Jeff.
c. The whole family appreciated the letter Senator Clinton sent to uncle Jeff.
d. The whole family appreciated the letter senator Clinton sent to uncle Jeff.

36. Identify the sentence that uses capitalization correctly.
   a. On Friday, it was Chinese New Year, so we went to Yien's restaurant to celebrate.
   b. On friday, it was Chinese new year, so we went to Yien's Restaurant to celebrate.
   c. On Friday, it was Chinese New Year, so we went to Yien's Restaurant to celebrate.
   d. On Friday, it was Chinese new year, so we went to Yien's restaurant to celebrate.

37. Identify the sentence that uses capitalization correctly.
   a. I plan to go to Canada this summer to watch the Calgary stampede.
   b. I plan to go to canada this Summer to watch the Calgary Stampede.
   c. I plan to go to Canada this summer to watch the Calgary Stampede.
   d. I plan to go to Canada this Summer to watch the Calgary Stampede.

38. Identify the correct word for the blank in the following sentence.
   We parked ____, but we still received a ticket.
   a. Legally
   b. legally

39. Which of the following sentences is punctuated correctly?
   a. My appt. with Dr. Nayel is at 5:15 P.M.
   b. My appt. with Dr Nayel is at 5:15 P.M.
   c. My appt. with Dr. Nayel is at 5:15 PM.
   d. My appt with Dr. Nayel is at 5:15 PM

40. Which of the following sentences is punctuated correctly?
   a. Have the paychecks arrived yet.
   b. Have the paychecks arrived yet?
   b. Have the paychecks arrived yet!
   b. Have the paychecks, arrived yet?

41. Which of the following sentences is punctuated correctly?
   a. Sadly, I walked home.
   b. Sadly I walked home.
   c. Sadly I walked, home.
   d. Sadly, I walked, home.

42. Which of the following sentences is punctuated correctly?
   a. When Yoshiro saw the beautiful cabin; by the lake, he was happy too.
   b. When Yoshiro saw the beautiful, cabin by the lake he was happy, too.
   c. When Yoshiro saw the beautiful cabin, by the lake, he was happy, too.
   d. When Yoshiro saw the beautiful cabin by the lake, he was happy, too.

43. Which of the following sentences is punctuated correctly?
   a. Ms. Lundquist my second grade teacher has written a very helpful book.
   b. Ms. Lundquist my second grade teacher, has written a very helpful book.
   c. Ms. Lundquist, my second grade teacher, has written a very helpful book.
   d. Ms. Lundquist, my second grade teacher has written a very helpful book.

44. Which of the following sentences is punctuated correctly?
   a. The Little League baseball fields near San Diego California are clean and well-lit.
   b. The Little League baseball fields near San Diego, California, are clean and well-lit.
   c. The Little League baseball fields near San Diego, California are clean and well-lit.
   d. The Little League baseball fields near San Diego, California are clean, and well-lit.

45. Which of the following sentences is punctuated correctly?

  a. At 3:45 P.M., Freddy will umpire the varsity game, Tomas, the junior varsity game, and Federico, the freshman game.

  b. At 345 PM, Freddy will umpire the varsity game; Tomas, the junior varsity game; and Federico, the freshman game.

  c. At 3:45 P.M. Freddy, will umpire the varsity game, Tomas, the junior varsity game, and Federico, the freshman game.

  d. At 3:45 P.M., Freddy will umpire the varsity game; Tomas, the junior varsity game; and Federico, the freshman game.

46. Which of the following sentences is punctuated correctly?

  a. The bookstore had to move its collection of children's books.

  b. The bookstore had to move it's collection of childrens' books.

  c. The bookstore had to move its' collection of children's books.

  d. The bookstore had to move its' collection of childrens' books.

47. Which of the following sentences is punctuated correctly?

  a. The professor asked, "Has anybody read 'A Good Man Is Hard to Find'?"

  b. The professor asked "has anybody read 'A Good Man Is Hard to Find'?"

  c. The professor asked, "Has anybody read "A Good Man Is Hard to Find"?"

  d. The professor asked, "has anybody read 'A Good Man Is Hard to Find?' "

48. Which of the following sentences is punctuated correctly?

  a. All thirty two nine year old students carried twenty pound backpacks.

  b. All thirty-two nine year old students carried twenty-pound backpacks.

  c. All thirty two nine-year-old students carried twenty-pound-backpacks.

  d. All thirty-two nine-year-old students carried twenty-pound backpacks.

49. Identify the correct words for the blank in the following sentence.

  I would like to have the party ____ more ____ at a restaurant.

  a. hear, than

  b. hear, then

  c. here, than

  d. here, then

50. Identify the correct words for the blanks in the following sentence.

  We ____ put on our uniforms, but we still ____ late for the game.

  a. already, maybe

  b. already, may be

  c. all ready, maybe

  d. all ready, may be

► Answers

1. b. Lesson 2	**26.** a. Lesson 10
2. c. Lesson 2	**27.** b. Lesson 10
3. a. Lesson 2	**28.** a. Lesson 10
4. a. Lesson 3	**29.** b. Lesson 11
5. d. Lesson 3	**30.** a. Lesson 11
6. a. Lesson 3	**31.** b. Lesson 11
7. c. Lesson 4	**32.** b. Lesson 11
8. d. Lesson 4	**33.** b. Lesson 11
9. b. Lesson 4	**34.** d. Lesson 12
10. d. Lesson 5	**35.** a. Lesson 12
11. c. Lesson 5	**36.** c. Lesson 12
12. c. Lesson 6	**37.** c. Lesson 12
13. d. Lesson 6	**38.** b. Lesson 12
14. a. Lesson 7	**39.** a. Lesson 13
15. b. Lesson 7	**40.** b. Lesson 13
16. c. Lesson 7	**41.** a. Lesson 14
17. a. Lesson 7	**42.** d. Lesson 14
18. d. Lesson 8	**43.** c. Lesson 14
19. b. Lesson 8	**44.** c. Lesson 14
20. c. Lesson 8	**45.** d. Lesson 15
21. b. Lesson 9	**46.** a. Lesson 16
22. a. Lesson 9	**47.** a. Lesson 17
23. b. Lesson 9	**48.** d. Lesson 18
24. a. Lesson 9	**49.** c. Lesson 19
25. a. Lesson 9	**50.** b. Lesson 19

1 ▶ Understanding the Writing Process

LESSON SUMMARY

In order to proofread, revise, and edit you need to understand the writing process—from prewriting to drafting, editing, revising, and writing a final draft. This lesson discusses the writing steps and then gives you strategies to help you write the best possible final draft.

The writing process has only just begun when you write the last word of your first draft. It is in the process of revising and editing that the draft takes shape and becomes a crafted piece of writing. Writing is an art, and like any good artist, a good writer continues to work on a piece until it has the desired impact.

▶ Prewriting/Brainstorming

First, it is important to figure out what you know about a topic. Since many ideas come to mind when you begin to think about a topic, take time to write them down. First thoughts are easily forgotten if they are not committed to paper. You can do this with a prewriting technique such as brainstorming, clustering, mapping, or listing. You can use graphic organizers like charts, story maps, diagrams, or a cluster like the example on the next page.

Prewriting can take place in all sorts of inconvenient locations, and you may only have a napkin, a piece of scrap paper, or an envelope on which to write. Just don't think a napkin with scribbles on it is the final draft. You still have much work to do.

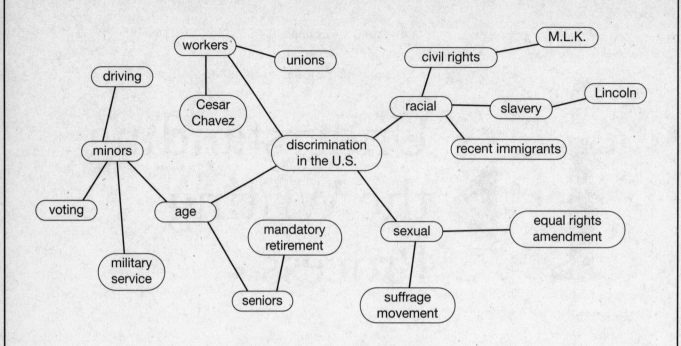

▶ Drafting

The next step is turning those thoughts into a first draft. Those of you who skip the prewriting step and jump right into a first draft will find that the editing stage takes more time than it should. You may even find that you have changed your mind from the beginning to the end of a piece, or that the first paragraph is spent getting ready to say something. That's fine, but be prepared to reorganize your entire draft.

Writing with a plan makes the entire writing process easier. Imagine you are a famous writer of mystery novels. If you don't know *whodunit*, how can you write the chapters that lead up to the part where the detective reveals the culprit? It is the same with your writing. Without an organizational plan, the paper you write may not take the right shape and may not say all you intended to say.

▶ Revising As You Go

Most writers revise as they write. That's why pencils with erasers were invented. If you are a writer who uses pen and paper, feel free to fill your first drafts with arrows and crossed-out words. You may continue a sentence down the margin or on the back of the page, or use asterisks to remind you of where you want to go back and add an idea or edit a sentence.

If you use a computer to compose, use symbols to remind you of changes that need to be made. Put a questionable sentence in **boldface** or a different color so you can remember to return to it later. A short string of unusual marks like #@$*%! will also catch your eye and remind you to return to a trouble spot. Typing them may even relieve some of the tension you're feeling as you struggle with your draft. Just remember that if you're planning to show your draft to someone, like a teacher or coworker, you may want to clean it up a little first.

Computers also make it easier to make changes as you go, but remember that a computer's grammar check or spell check is not foolproof. Computers do not understand the subtle nuances of our living language. A well-trained proofreader or editor can.

▶ Proofreading

Proofreading is simply careful reading. As you review every word, sentence, and paragraph, you *will* find errors. When you locate them, you can use proofreading symbols to shorten the amount of time you spend editing. It is an excellent idea to become familiar with these symbols. At the bottom of this page are a few examples of the most common ones, but be sure to check Appendix A for a complete list.

Of course, in order to find errors, you must know what they are. Read on to discover the culprits that can sabotage a good piece of writing.

▶ Capitalization and Punctuation

Capitalization and punctuation are like auto mechanics for your writing. They tune up your sentences and make them start, stop, and run smoothly.

Example

the russian Ballet travel's. all over the world, Performing to amazed Audiences. in each new city;

This sentence jerks along like an old car driven by someone who doesn't know how to use the brakes.

Edited Example

The Russian Ballet travels all over the world, performing to amazed audiences in each new city.

Every sentence begins with a capital letter. That's the easy part. Many other words are capitalized, too, however, and those rules can be harder to remember. Lesson 12 reviews all the rules of capitalization for you.

While every sentence begins with a capital letter, every sentence ends with some sort of punctuation. The proper use of end marks like periods, exclamation points, and question marks (Lesson 13) and other punctuation like commas, colons, semicolons, apostrophes, and quotation marks (Lessons 14–17) will help your reader make sense of your words. Punctuation is often the difference between a complete sentence and a sentence fragment or run-on (Lesson 2). Other punctuation marks like hyphens, dashes, and ellipses (Lesson 18)

SYMBOL	EXAMPLE	MEANING OF SYMBOL
≡	Stevenson High school	Capitalize a lower-case letter.
/	the $\cancel{S}$econd string	Make a capital letter lower-case.
∧	Go ∧ at the light. *(right)*	Insert a missing word, letter, or punctuation mark.
ℽ	I had an ~~an~~ idea	Delete a word, letter, or punctuation mark.
∩	rec⁀ieve	Change the order of the letters.
⊙	. . . to the end⊙	Add a period.
⋀	. . . apples⋀oranges, and . . .	Add a comma.

give flare to your writing and should be used for function as well as style.

► Spelling

Correct spelling gives your work credibility. Not only will your reader know that you are educated, but also that you are careful about your work. You should have a dictionary handy to confirm that you have correctly spelled all unfamiliar words, especially if they are key words in the piece. In the workplace, a memo with a repeatedly misspelled word can be embarrassing. An essay with a misspelled word in the title, or a word that is spelled incorrectly throughout the piece, can affect your final grade. Avoid embarrassing situations like these by checking your spelling.

Even if you know all the spelling rules by heart, you will come across exceptions to the rules. Words that come from other languages (bourgeois, psyche), have silent letters (dumb, knack), or are technical terms (cryogenics, chimerical) can present problems. In addition, the spelling can change when the word is made plural (puppies, octopi). Homonyms like *bear/bare* or *course/coarse* can be easily confused, as can words that have unusual vowel combinations (beauty, archaeology). When in doubt, check it out by consulting a dictionary.

► Spell Check Programs

If you use a computer, most word processing programs contain a spell check and a dictionary, so use them. Just be aware that spell check doesn't always provide the right answer, so double-check your choices. If your spell check gives three suggestions, you will have to consult a dictionary for the right one.

Example
He read *thru* the entire paper looking for a story on the protest march.

Spell check suggests replacing "thru" with "through," "threw," or "thorough." The dictionary will tell you that the correct spelling is "through."

Choosing a suggested spelling from spell check that is incorrect in the context of your sentence can affect an entire piece. As teachers and employers become more familiar with spell check programs, they learn to recognize when a writer has relied on spell check. For example, homonyms such as *pane* and *pain* and commonly confused words, such as *where, wear,* and *were* (Lesson 19) present a problem for spell check, just as they do for many writers. Ultimately, there is no substitute for a dictionary and a set of trained eyes and ears.

► Grammar

Unfortunately, there is no "grammar dictionary," but there are thousands of reliable grammar handbooks. In order to communicate in standard written English, you have to pay attention to the rules. You need to understand the parts of speech when you write, and you have to combine them properly.

Example
The dance team felt that they had performed bad.

"Bad" in this form is an adjective, and adjectives modify nouns. The word "bad" must be replaced by an adverb to modify the verb *had performed*. To turn *bad* into an adverb, you must add the ending *-ly*.

Edited Example
The dance team felt that they had performed badly.

One of the best ways to check for grammatical errors is to read your writing aloud. When you read silently, your eyes make automatic corrections, or may skip over mistakes. Your ears aren't as easily fooled, however, and will catch many of your mistakes. If you are in a situation where you can't read aloud, try whispering or mouthing the words as you read. If something doesn't sound right, check the grammar.

▶ Grammar Check

Computers that use grammar check programs cannot find every error. Grammar check will highlight any sentence that has a potential error, and you should examine it. The program is helpful for correcting some basic grammatical issues, but it also functions in other ways. Many grammar check programs flag sentences in the passive voice (Lesson 8), which is a style choice. While the passive voice is not wrong, it can lead to some very flat and sometimes confusing writing. It may be a good idea to change some of the passive verbs to active ones.

Many programs also highlight sentence fragments and sentences that are over 50 words long (Lesson 2). Sentence fragments are never correct grammatically, although they may be used intentionally in certain informal situations.

It is important to remember that not only do grammar check programs sometimes point out sentences that are correct, but they also do not always catch sentences that are incorrect.

Example
I have one pairs of pants.

Edited Example
I have one pair of pants.

There is no substitute for understanding the rules governing grammar and careful proofreading.

▶ Editing

Once you are finished proofreading, you will probably need to cut words out of your piece in some places and add more material in other places. Repetitive words or phrases and awkward or wordy sentences (Lesson 3) can be edited. If you begin to write without an organizational plan, you may have to cut some good-sized chunks from your writing because they wander from the main idea. You may also need to expand ideas that you did not explain fully in your first draft. Editing is about streamlining your piece. Good writing is clear, concise, and to the point.

▶ Revision

Reading your writing a few times allows you to work on different aspects of your piece. Some revision takes place as you write, and some takes place after you have read the whole piece and are able to see if it works. Most writers revise more than once, and many writers proofread and edit each draft.

If your draft has errors that make it difficult to understand, you should start by proofreading. Print out your paper, mark it with proofreading symbols, and make any necessary corrections in grammar or mechanics. Proofreading and editing can help make your meaning clear, and clarity makes your piece easier to understand.

If your draft is cohesive, you can concentrate more on the big picture. Are your paragraphs in the right order? Do they make sense and work together? Are your transitions smooth and your conclusions strong? Have you avoided sounding wishy-washy or too aggressive? Is the voice too passive? Some writers prefer to think about these issues during the first reading. Others proofread, edit, and rearrange while they read the draft. It doesn't matter which approach you use, but plan to read each draft at least twice. Read it once focusing on the big picture, and once focusing on the smaller details of the piece.

Real revision is the process of transforming a piece; the results of your revisions may not look much like your first draft at all. Even if you start with an organizational plan, it is possible that you will decide that the piece needs to be reorganized only after you have written an entire draft. If the piece is research-based, discovering new information can require a completely new treatment of the subject. If your piece is supposed to be persuasive, maybe you will discover it is not persuasive enough.

Thinking of your writing as a work in progress is the ideal approach. Writing and revising several drafts takes time, however, and time is a luxury many writers do not have. Perhaps you have a pressing due date or an important meeting. You can still improve your writing in a short period of time.

One strategy for revising is to create an outline from your draft. This may sound like you are working backward because usually the outline precedes the draft, but even if you originally worked from an outline, this second outline can be helpful. Read your writing and summarize each paragraph with a word or short phrase. Write this summary in the margin of your draft. When you have done this for the entire piece, list the summary words or phrases on a separate sheet. If you originally worked from an outline, how do the list and outline compare? If you did not work from an outline, can you see places where re-ordering paragraphs might help? You may want to move three or four paragraphs and see if this improves the piece.

"Cut and paste" editing like this is easy to do on a computer. In a word processing program, you can highlight, cut, and paste sentences and whole paragraphs. If you are uneasy or afraid you may destroy your draft, you may want to choose "select all" and copy your work into a new blank document just so your original draft is safe and accessible. Now, you can experiment a little with moving and changing your text.

If you are working with a handwritten draft, making a photocopy is a good way to revise without destroying the original. Remember to double-space or skip lines on the first draft to give yourself room to revise. To move paragraphs, simply number them and read them in your new order. If you are working from a copy, take out your scissors and literally cut the paragraphs into pieces. Instead of using glue or paste, use tape, or thumbtack the pieces to a bulletin board. That way you can continue to move the pieces around until they are in an order that works best for you. No matter how you approach revising, it is a valuable part of the writing process. Don't be afraid to rearrange whole paragraphs and fine-tune your tone, voice, and style (Lesson 7) as you revise.

▶ Tone

The tone of the piece is the way in which the writer conveys his or her attitude or purpose. The tone is the "sound" of your writing, and the words you choose affect the way your writing sounds. If you use qualifying words (Lesson 3) like "I believe" and "to a certain extent," your piece has a less confident tone. If you use imperative words like "must" and "absolutely," your piece sounds assertive. Just like the tone of your speaking voice, your tone when you write can be angry, joyful, commanding, or indifferent.

If you are writing about a topic in which you are emotionally invested, the tone of your first draft may be too strong. Be sure to consider your audience and purpose and adjust the tone through revision.

For example, if you bought a CD player and it broke the next day, you would probably be upset. If the salesperson refused to refund your money, you would definitely be upset. A first draft of a letter to the store manager might help you sort out your complaint, but if your purpose is to receive a refund, your first draft might be too angry and accusatory. It is a business letter, after all. A second draft, in which you keep your audience (the store manager) and your purpose (to get a refund) in mind, should clearly state the situation and the service you expect to receive.

▶ Slang

The words you choose make a big difference. If your piece of writing is an assignment for school, it should use language that is appropriate for an educational setting. If it is for work, it should use language that is professional. The secret is to know your audience. Slang is not appropriate in an academic piece, but it can give a creative short story a more realistic tone.

Slang is language that is specific to a group of people. When we think of slang, we usually think of young people, but every generation has its slang. Have you heard the terms "23 Skidoo" or "Top Drawer" or "The Cat's Pajamas?" These words are American slang from the 1920s—the ones that your grandfather may have used when he was young. If these old-fashioned phrases were used in your favorite magazine, you probably would not understand them. On the other hand, Grandpa is probably not going to read the magazine that discusses "New Jack's gettin' real." Slang has a use, but it tends to alienate people who do not understand it.

Colloquialisms and dialect are inappropriate for certain types of writing as well. The stock market predictions that you write for your brokerage firm should not declare, "I am so not gonna recommend blue chip stocks to every Tom, Dick, and Harry." It should say, "Blue chip stocks are not recommended for everyone." In an academic or work-related piece, it is safest to write in proper English in order to appeal to the largest audience.

▶ Voice

Voice can be *active* or *passive*, depending on your choice of verbs (see Lesson 8). Most pieces work better using the active voice. Like a well-made action movie, an active voice grabs the audience's attention. The subject of the sentence becomes a "hero" who performs courageous feats and death-defying acts with action verbs like *flying*, *running*, and *capturing*.

The passive voice has a purpose, also. It is used to express a state of being. Where would we be without the passive verb "to be?" The appropriate verb in a sentence could very well be *am, are,* or *have been*. The passive voice should also be used when the writer doesn't know or doesn't want to state who performed the action.

Example
The purse was stolen.

In this case, no one knows who stole the purse, so the active voice would not work.

▶ Style

Style is the particular way in which you express yourself in writing. It is the craft of your writing, and is the product of careful revision. It is the combination of voice, tone, and word choice, in which all the parts of writing—language, rhythm, even grammar—come together to make your writing unique.

Style should be your goal when you revise. Find changes that will make each sentence an important part of the whole. Tinker with your words until your language becomes accurate and clear. As in fashion, one little "accessory" can be the difference between an average outfit and a real eye-catcher. Style is always recognizable, and good style will make others take note of what you have to say.

Summary

Following the advice in this book will help you learn to proofread, edit, and revise your writing. As a writer, you should remember to keep important tools handy. A dictionary, a grammar handbook, and a thesaurus are essential. Remember: Write often, proofread carefully, edit judiciously, and revise until you are satisfied.

2 ▶ Writing Sentences

LESSON SUMMARY

In this lesson, you will look at the parts of a sentence, learn to spot complete and incomplete sentences, and revise sentence fragments and run-on sentences.

Successful writing means putting sentences together precisely. It can be compared to baking. If you don't follow the recipe or if you leave out a key ingredient, the cake will not turn out right. To ensure baking success, it is important to follow a recipe. To ensure writing success, it is important to know that sentences have recipes too. As you proofread, edit, and revise your work, remember that the basic recipe is very simple: Combine one subject with one predicate to yield one complete thought.

Examples

Bears stand in cold mountain streams.

Subject   *Predicate*

The girl ate macaroni and cheese.

Subject   *Predicate*

Sometimes the predicate appears first in the sentence.

Example
Lucky are the few who survived the Battle of the

Predicate   Subject

Bulge.

▶ Simple Subjects and Simple Predicates

Subjects are nouns (a person, place, thing, or idea). The simple subject is the key word in the sentence. The subject of the sentence can appear almost anywhere in the sentence, so it can often be difficult to locate. One strategy for finding the subject is to find the verb (an action or linking word) or predicate first.

Example
The children carved the pumpkins.

Carved is the verb in this sentence. When you ask "Who or what did the carving?" the answer is *children*, so *children* is the subject.

Example
Down the street rolled the car.

The verb in the example sentence is *rolled.* Who or what rolled? The answer is *car,* so *car* is the subject.

The verb that you identify is the simple predicate—the main action of the subject. Just as the simple subject is the key noun in a sentence, the simple predicate is the key verb. The verb can be one word or a verb phrase such as *are jumping, will jump, has jumped, might have jumped,* etc. When the verb is a phrase, all parts of the verb phrase make up the simple predicate.

Example
Juan has ridden his bicycle to work.

In the example sentence, the simple predicate is *has ridden.*

▶ Compound Subjects and Compound Predicates

A sentence can have more than one subject that uses the same verb. When there are two subjects connected by *and, or,* or *nor,* they are called compound subjects.

Example
Manuel and Jonathan held the flag.

The compound subject in the example sentence is *Manuel and Jonathan.*

A sentence can have a compound predicate, also connected by *and, or,* or *nor.*

Example
Julian cannot speak or read French.

The compound predicate is *speak or read.*

Exercise 1
Underline the subject once and the predicate twice in the following sentences. Remember, it is often easier to find the predicate (verb, or action word) first and then the subject (the noun that is performing the action). Answers can be found at the end of the lesson.

1. Larry ate the sushi.

2. Akiko changed the diaper.

3. In the haunted house went the children.

4. Bobby and Devone sat in their chairs.

5. Campbell fished and hunted in the Cascade Mountains.

6. They were running to catch the bus.

7. Mary and Al skipped the previews and watched only the feature presentation.

8. Adam and I made a soap box derby car.

9. The paper route was taking too long.

10. The building and the house caught on fire.

▶ Objects

The *direct object* of a sentence is the part of the predicate that is receiving the action of the verb or shows the result of the action. For example, if the subject of a sentence is *Mary*, and the verb is *throws*, you need an object—*what* Mary throws.

Example
Nina brought a present to the birthday party.

The subject of the sentence is *Nina*, the verb is *brought*, and the object is *present*.

Some sentences also contain an *indirect object*, which tells to whom or for whom the action of the verb is done and who is receiving the direct object. A sentence must have a direct object in order to have an indirect object. A common type of indirect object is an *object of a preposition.*. Prepositions are words such as *to*, *with*, *of*, *by*, *from*, *between*, and *among*.

Example
Nina gave a present to Sarah.

This sentence has two objects—a direct object, *present*, and an indirect object, *Sarah*.

You will read more about objects in Lesson 10, which discusses pronoun agreement and the proper use of the objective case.

▶ Clauses

Together, the subject and predicate make up a clause. If the clause expresses a complete thought, it is an independent clause. Independent clauses can stand alone as complete sentences, as you can see in the following examples.

Examples
The team won the game.
Amy and Georgia live in New Mexico.

If the clause does not express a complete thought, it is not a complete sentence and is called a dependent or subordinate clause. Dependent or subordinate clauses are often incorrectly separated from the sentence where they belong. When this happens, a sentence fragment is created, as you can see in the following examples.

Example
though I was tired

Example
when he caught his breath

▶ Sentence Fragments

Sentence fragments do not make complete sentences all by themselves. Often they occur as a result of faulty punctuation. If you put a period in the wrong place, before a complete thought is expressed, you will create a fragment. If you omit a subject or predicate, you will also create a sentence fragment.

Example
FRAGMENT: I thought I saw. The new teacher taking the bus.
To correct this example, simply change the punctuation.
COMPLETE THOUGHT: I thought I saw the new teacher taking the bus.

Example
FRAGMENT: "An American in Paris." A great movie.
To correct this example, you must add a predicate or verb.
COMPLETE THOUGHT: "An American in Paris" is a great movie.

Exercise 2

Proofread and revise the following sentence fragments. Make them complete sentences by adding the missing subject or predicate. Write the revised sentences on the lines provided. *Note:* There may be many ways to revise the sentences depending on the words you choose to add. Some need both a subject and a predicate. Try to make them the best sentences you can, and don't forget to add the appropriate end punctuation. Answers can be found at the end of the lesson.

11. Ran for student body president

_____

12. Was wearing my shin guards

_____

13. Luis to Puerto Rico rather frequently

_____

14. Chose the new soccer team captains, Michael and Jose

_____

_____

15. Played the electric guitar in her new band

_____

16. Sent me an e-mail with a virus

_____

17. The cat while she ate

_____

18. After the accident happened in front of the school

_____

_____

19. Put too much syrup on his pancakes

_____

20. Rarely gets up before noon on Saturdays

_____

Sentence fragments also occur when a subordinating conjunction—like *after, although, as, as much as, because, before, how, if, in order that, inasmuch as, provided, since, than, though, that, unless, until, when, where, while*—precedes an independent clause.

Example

FRAGMENT: Until the players began stretching.

This sentence fragment can be remedied by either eliminating the conjunction, or by adding a clause to the fragment to form a complete thought.

COMPLETE THOUGHT: The players began stretching.

COMPLETE THOUGHT: Until the players began stretching, they had many pulled muscles.

Coordinating conjunctions—like *and, but, or, nor,* and *for*—are often a quick fix for both sentence fragments and run-on sentences.

Example

FRAGMENT: The newspaper and a loaf of bread on your way home.

COMPLETE THOUGHT: Pick up the newspaper and a loaf of bread on your way home.

Exercise 3

Proofread and revise the following sentences and then add the proper punctuation. Write the revised sentences on the lines provided. Answers can be found at the end of the lesson.

21. After we saw the movie. We went to the café and discussed it.

_____

_____

22. Because the announcer spoke quickly. We didn't understand.

_____

_____

23. Our basketball team won the state title. Three years in a row.

_____

_____

24. Although Oregon is a beautiful state. It tends to rain a lot.

_____

_____

25. The two-point conversion. Made football games more exciting.

_____

_____

26. Sewing the Halloween costume. I stuck my finger with the needle.

_____

_____

27. Unless you know how to drive a manual transmission car. Buy an automatic.

_____

_____

28. Because dock workers had no contract. They discussed going on strike.

_____

_____

29. After the concert was over. I bought a T-shirt of the band.

_____

_____

30. Since we had eaten a big breakfast. We just snacked the rest of the day.

_____

_____

Exercise 4

Proofread and revise the following sentence fragments so that they form complete sentences. Write the revised sentences on the lines provided. Answers can be found at the end of the lesson.

31. While the taxi driver drove faster

_____

32. My daughter. After she wrote a letter

_____

33. Before we start the show

_____

34. When Andrew gave his closing argument

_____

35. Unless you would like Olga to buy them for you

_____

_____

36. Antonio is tired. Because he just moved again

_____

37. Jose played soccer. Although he had never played before

_____

_____

38. Since Tom has a new class

_____

39. The crowd cheered. When the union leader finished his speech

_____

_____

40. After our lunch of tuna fish sandwiches

_____

▶ Run-On Sentences

Run-on sentences are like the person at the all-you-can-eat buffet who overfills a plate when he or she could have simply gone back for a second helping. Run-on sentences are two or more independent clauses written as though they were one sentence. The main cause of run-on sentences, like fragments, is faulty punctuation. End marks like periods, exclamation points, and question marks (Lesson 13) can make or break a sentence.

Example
This run-on sentence is missing punctuation:
RUN-ON: Julie studies hard she is trying to win a fellowship next year.

CORRECT: Julie studies hard. She is trying to win a fellowship next year.

Semicolons (Lesson 15) can also be used to revise run-on sentences..

Example
RUN-ON: The soccer game ended at four, it was too late to go to the birthday party.
CORRECT: The soccer game ended at four; it was too late to go to the birthday party.

Commas, when used with a conjunction, can transform run-on sentences. Conjunctions come in three types: coordinating, correlative, and subordinating. Coordinating conjunctions (*and, but, or, nor, so, for, yet*) can be used to correct run-on sentences.

Example
RUN-ON: Gillian lived in Portland she lived in New York.
CORRECT: Gillian lived in Portland, and she lived in New York.

Correlative conjunctions (*both . . . and, neither . . . nor, not only . . . but also, whether . . . or, either . . . or*) join similar kinds of items and are always used in pairs.

Example
RUN-ON: They saw aquatic animals like moray eels and sharks they saw gorillas and chimpanzees.
CORRECT: They not only saw aquatic animals like moray eels and sharks, but they also saw gorillas and chimpanzees.

Subordinating conjunctions (*after, although, as far as, as if, as long as, as soon as, as though, because, before, if, in order that, provided that, since, so that, than, that, unless, until, when, whenever, where, wherever, whether, while*) join clauses with the rest of a sentence.

Example
RUN-ON: Isabel sang I played music.
CORRECT: When I played music, Isabel sang.

Exercise 5

Add end marks, commas, or semi-colons to fix the following sentences. Write the revised sentences on the lines provided. Answers can be found at the end of the lesson.

41. Will you come to the party we think you'll have fun.

_____

_____

42. We spent a year traveling in Asia, consequently, we speak some Chinese.

_____

_____

43. The Avinas live on Old Germantown Road, they've lived there for thirty years.

_____

_____

44. Powdered fruit drinks taste good, nevertheless, they are not as nutritious as juice.

_____

_____

45. Mrs. Michaels introduced me to the reading instructor. A neighbor of mine.

_____

_____

46. I sent her flowers. Hoping she would forgive me.

_____

_____

47. Neil locked the gate then we left the ranch.

_____

48. I found it therefore I get to keep it.

_____

49. The flag has thirteen stripes. As most U.S. citizens know.

_____

_____

50. The hockey team also travels to southern states. Such as Texas and Louisiana.

_____

_____

Sometimes, run-on sentences occur when writers use adverbs such as _then, however,_ or _therefore_ as if they were conjunctions. This type of error is easily fixed. By using correct punctuation—such as a semicolon—or by making two sentences out of one run-on, the writing takes the correct shape and form.

Example
RUN-ON: I bought a new motorcycle however my license had expired.
CORRECT: I bought a new motorcycle; however, my license had expired.

CORRECT: I bought a new motorcycle. However, my license had expired.

▶ Types of Sentences

A simple sentence contains only one independent clause and is typically short. If you write with only simple sentences, your writing will not have the variety and complexity of good writing. As you learn to vary your sentences by using compound, complex, and compound-complex sentences, you will find that you are able to express more complex relationships between ideas.

A compound sentence contains more than one independent clause and no subordinate clauses.

Example
The children couldn't finish the race,
    Independent clause
but the adults could easily.
    Independent clause

A complex sentence contains only one independent clause and at least one subordinate clause.

Example
As soon as we sat at the table,
    Subordinate clause
the waiter brought menus.
    Independent clause

A compound-complex sentence contains more than one independent clause and at least one subordinate clause.

Example
When Danny finally enrolled in college,
    Subordinate clause
he studied very hard,
    Independent clause
for he had missed the first two weeks of classes.
    Independent clause

Remember, compound, complex, and compound-complex sentences add depth to your writing, but they need to be punctuated correctly or they become run-on sentences. If you use only simple sentences, your writing sounds very choppy. Simple sentences are short. They say one thing. They don't give much detail. They don't flow. A good piece of writing uses both short and long sentences (see Lesson 4) for variety. When you write, alternating the length of sentences is a good idea, as long as the short sentences aren't fragments and the long sentences aren't run-ons.

Exercise 6

Fix the following sentence fragments and run-on sentences by adding a conjunction and any necessary punctuation. Write the revised sentence on the lines provided. Answers can be found at the end of the lesson.

51. I wanted to buy a bicycle. My paycheck wasn't enough.

_____

_____

52. I ate the ice cream my stomach hurt.

_____

53. I wore my new shoes I got blisters.

_____

54. You play the guitar. I practice my singing.

_____

55. It rains. The field turns to mud.

_____

56. I can't have dessert I eat my dinner.

_____

57. I finish my homework I am going to watch T.V.

_____

_____

58. There's a need. We will be there to help out.

_____

59. I made the bed my room passed inspection.

_____

60. You can fix my broken alarm clock you can buy me a new one.

_____

Summary

Knowing the parts of a sentence and the kinds of sentences that are a part of good writing will help you proofread, revise, and edit your work. As you examine your own writing, mark the places where faulty punctuation has created sentence fragments or run-on sentences. Revise them by using proper end marks, semicolons, or conjunctions.

▶ Answers

Exercise 1

1. subject = Larry; predicate = ate
2. subject = Akiko; predicate = changed
3. subject = children; predicate = went
4. subjects = Bobby, Devone; predicate = sat
5. subject = Campbell; predicate = fished, hunted
6. subject = They; predicate = were running
7. subjects = Mary, Al; predicate = skipped, watched
8. subjects = Adam, I; predicate = made
9. subject = route; predicate = was taking
10. subjects = building, house; predicate = caught

Exercise 2

11. Add a subject, i.e. <u>Andy</u> ran for student body president.
12. Add a subject, i.e. <u>I</u> was wearing my shin guards.
13. Add a predicate, i.e. Luis <u>flew</u> to Puerto Rico rather frequently.
14. Add a subject, i.e. <u>The team</u> chose the new soccer team captains, Michael and Jose.
15. Add a subject, i.e. <u>Ellen</u> played the electric guitar in her new band.
16. Add a subject, i.e. <u>Pete</u> sent me an e-mail with a virus.
17. Add a predicate, i.e. The cat <u>twitched</u> while she ate.
18. Add both a subject and a predicate, i.e. <u>The police arrived</u> after the accident happened in front of the school.
19. Add a subject, i.e. <u>Brad</u> put too much syrup on his pancakes.
20. Add a subject, i.e. <u>Stacy</u> rarely gets up before noon on Saturdays.

Exercise 3

21. After we saw the movie, we went to the café and discussed it.
22. Because the announcer spoke quickly, we didn't understand.
23. Our basketball team won the state title three years in a row.
24. Although Oregon is a beautiful state, it tends to rain a lot.
25. The two-point conversion made football games more exciting.
26. Sewing the Halloween costume, I stuck my finger with the needle.
27. Unless you know how to drive a manual transmission car, buy an automatic.
28. Because dock workers had no contract, they discussed going on strike.
29. After the concert was over, I bought a T-shirt of the band.
30. Since we had eaten a big breakfast, we just snacked the rest of the day.

Exercise 4

31. Needs an independent clause attached, i.e. While the taxi driver drove faster, we held on.
32. Needs a predicate, i.e. My daughter sighed after she wrote a letter.
33. Needs an independent clause attached, i.e. Before we start the show, we should warm up our voices.
34. Needs an independent clause attached, i.e. When Andrew gave his closing argument, the courtroom was silent.
35. Needs an independent clause attached, i.e. You should buy them unless you would like Olga to buy them for you.
36. Needs the punctuation fixed, i.e. Antonio is tired because he just moved again.
37. Needs the punctuation fixed, i.e. Jose played soccer although he had never played before.

38. Needs an independent clause attached, i.e. Since Tom has a new class, his schedule is full.

39. Needs the punctuation fixed, i.e. The crowd cheered when the union leader finished his speech.

40. Needs an independent clause attached, i.e. After our lunch of tuna fish sandwiches, we had coffee.

Exercise 5

41. Will you come to the party? We think you'll have fun.

42. We spent a year traveling in Asia; consequently, we speak some Chinese.

43. The Avinas live on Old Germantown Road. They've lived there for thirty years.

44. Powdered fruit drinks taste good; nevertheless, they are not as nutritious as juice.

45. Mrs. Michaels introduced me to the reading instructor, a neighbor of mine.

46. I sent her flowers hoping she would forgive me.

47. Neil locked the gate, then we left the ranch.

48. I found it; therefore, I get to keep it.

49. The flag has thirteen stripes, as most U.S. citizens know.

50. The hockey team also travels to southern states, such as Texas and Louisiana.

Exercise 6

51. I wanted to buy a bicycle but my paycheck wasn't enough.

52. I ate the ice cream and my stomach hurt.

53. I wore my new shoes and I got blisters.

54. You play the guitar while I practice my singing.

55. When it rains, the field turns to mud.

56. I can't have dessert until I eat my dinner.

57. After I finish my homework, I am going to watch T.V.

58. When there's a need, we will be there to help out.

59. I made the bed so my room passed inspection.

60. You can fix my broken alarm clock or you can buy me a new one.

3 ▶ Avoiding Awkward Sentences

LESSON SUMMARY

This lesson deals with identifying and revising awkward sentences. When sentences are so long that they are hard to follow or so short that they sound choppy, they need thorough revision. Careful and skillful revising techniques will give a piece of writing a natural rhythm and flow.

Too often, writers use poorly chosen, inappropriate, or unnecessary language that can confuse a reader. Like a carpenter who has a tool for every task, writers should have words in their writer's toolbox that fit every task. Selecting the words and the order in which they appear takes practice. In this chapter you will learn strategies for revising sentences that are awkward, carry on too long, or are too short and choppy.

▶ Words that Have Little or No Meaning

When we write, we sometimes take on the same habits we have when we speak. Words or phrases that have little or no meaning fill space when we talk but have limited use in writing. Words such as *kind of, actually, in particular, really, certain, various, virtually, individual, basically, generally, given,* and *practically* give our brains a chance to collect our thoughts when speaking. When writing, we should have our thoughts already collected because this helps convey ideas more efficiently.

Example
Procrastination actually makes certain people really unsuccessful more than virtually any other particular habit.

Edited Example
Procrastination makes people unsuccessful more than any other habit.

Example
I am of the opinion that we should not prohibit children from talking in the hallways entirely and completely.

Revised Example
We should allow children to talk in the hallways on occasion.

▶ Redundancy

Often, writing assignments require a minimum number of words. Because of this, it is tempting to use several words of description instead of one well-chosen word with the same meaning. This redundancy, however, makes sentences awkward and interrupts the flow to a piece of writing. To write effectively, you must eliminate words that simply rephrase other words for no purpose.

Example
The football team made *future* plans to *completely* concentrate on the *basic* fundamentals of each *individual* position.

Plans are always for the future; concentrating implies complete focus; fundamental means basic; and positions are individual. Therefore, the italicized words are unnecessary modifiers.

Edited Example
The football team made plans to concentrate on the fundamentals of each position.

Some other common redundancies include *whole entire, big fat, complete truth, terrible tragedy, pitch black, various different, true facts, free gift,* and *final outcome.*

Words also imply categories, so you can often eliminate a word that names a category.

Example
The dinosaurs that were green colored were few in number during that period in history.

Edited Example
There were few green dinosaurs during that period.

Periods, such as the one in the sentence, are always periods *in history.*

These doubled words often occur in phrases, and sometimes these phrases are clichés (Lesson 19).

Example
I hope you give this matter your full and complete attention.

Edited Example
I hope you give this matter your complete attention.

Some common doubled word phrases are *pick and choose, full and complete, hope and trust, any and all, true and accurate, each and every, basic and fundamental, hopes and desires,* and *first and foremost.* Often it works best to eliminate both words, but occasionally eliminating one of the two words works best.

▶ Negatives

Changing negatives to affirmatives also eliminates extra words. Look for sentences that use *not* and see if you can rewrite the sentence to make it affirmative.

Example
NEGATIVE: She wore a sweater that was not different than mine.

Edited Example
She wore the same sweater as mine.

Double negatives make your writing sound more confusing. Some words are negative by definition, such as the verbs *preclude, exclude, fail, reject, avoid, deny, prohibit,* and *refuse* and such prepositions (Lesson 4) as *against* or *without.* Using a combination of these negative words will make your point very difficult to understand.

Example
DOUBLE NEGATIVES: Without failing to refuse denying an invitation, you have not avoided precluding buying a gift.

Edited Example
By accepting an invitation, you have agreed to buy a gift.

Exercise 1

Edit the following wordy sentences by eliminating words that have little or no meaning, words that are repetitive, words implied by other words, or by changing negatives to affirmatives. Write your answers on the lines provided. Answers can be found at the end of the lesson.

1. Actually, a basic and fundamental part of cooking is making sure you don't have the wrong ingredients.

_____

_____

2. Each and every student deserves a fair and equal chance to try out for intramural sports.

_____

_____

3. First and foremost, the Board of Directors cannot make a decision without a consensus of opinion.

_____

_____

_____

4. At an earlier time today, my sister told me she would pick me up after the end of work.

_____

_____

5. Various different people in our office were not against moving the water cooler to a location that would be less difficult for everyone to reach.

_____

_____

_____

_____

6. One accidental mistake some beginning swimmers make is not remembering to kick.

_____

_____

▶ Qualifiers

The best writing requires confidence. Starting sentences with phrase such as *I feel, I think, I believe, in my opinion,* or *I am of the opinion that* can dilute what you have to say. Instead of using qualifying phrases like those, say exactly what you mean.

Examples
WITH QUALIFIER: I believe that homework should be eliminated.
WITHOUT QUALIFIER: Homework should be eliminated.
WITH QUALIFIER: I am of the opinion that bungee jumping should be an Olympic sport.
WITHOUT QUALIFIER: Bungee jumping should be an Olympic sport.

Without unnecessary qualifiers, your writing takes on a more confident tone.

You should also be careful not to over-use words such as *very, pretty, quite, rather, clearly, obviously, certainly, always, of course, indeed, inevitably,* and *invariably.* These words can be useful in helping you make your point, but if you are using powerful language to begin with, you may find they are cluttering up your sentences rather than strengthening them.

Example
The cheese clearly overpowered the pasta and, of course, made the dish rather difficult to eat.

Edited Example
The cheese overpowered the pasta and made the dish difficult to eat.

Exercise 2
Locate the unnecessary qualifiers in the following sentences. Eliminate them and rewrite the sentences on the lines provided. Answers can be found at the end of the lesson.

7. In certain respects, the telephone appears to have done more to change the way we communicate than almost any other invention.

_____

_____

_____

8. Obviously, the V-8 engine is very powerful, but it certainly isn't the only good engine design.

_____

_____

9. Several students inevitably fail, even though the curriculum is quite clear.

_____

_____

10. Apparently, scientists find it virtually impossible to estimate the size of the universe, but usually they can come pretty close.

_____

_____

_____

11. Clearly, the very best skiers almost always suffer rather serious injuries.

_____

_____

▶ Vocabulary

There is no substitute for an extensive vocabulary. The more words you know, the more able you are to replace whole phrases with one accurate word. Increase your vocabulary and you make your writing more powerful. Start by keeping a list of words that you do not know, list their definitions, and use them in your everyday life. Using *context clues* can also help you increase your vocabulary. When you see a word that you do not know, examine the words that surround it to see if you can discover the meaning. Often, a word can be deciphered by examining the clues the other words give.

Understanding word parts will help you understand words you do not know as well. Prefixes and suffixes have meanings that can change the definition of a word or its part of speech. Greek and Latin roots appear often in English, and the more roots that are familiar to you, the more words you can figure out in your reading and use in your writing.

A thesaurus can help you find words to use, but like spell check or grammar check, it can change your piece in ways you may not realize. Your voice (Lesson 7) can become inconsistent, or you can use words incorrectly.

Not all words offered in a thesaurus are exact synonyms. For example, if your piece repeats the word "freedom" too often, and you use a thesaurus to find a word to replace it, you would find "liberty." This would work if your sentence says, "Our founding fathers fought for *liberty*." "Freedom" and "liberty" do not mean exactly the same thing, but "fought for liberty" is probably close enough. In the thesaurus under "freedom," you would also find "looseness," which could possibly replace "freedom" if your sentence is discussing a piece of clothing. However, our founding fathers did not fight for "looseness." This is an extreme example, but it illustrates the point that not all words in the thesaurus will work in all situations.

A thesaurus does not help you replace phrases either, which is important when you are trying to shorten sentences. Some common phrases can be shortened: *in the event that* becomes *if*; *concerning the matter of* becomes *about*; *are in a position* becomes *can*; *the reason for* becomes *why*; *because of the fact* becomes *because*.

Example
In the event that every union member decides to vote, we will have a huge turnout.

Edited Example
If every union member decides to vote, we will have a huge turnout.

Try to find the clearest way to write by eliminating unnecessary words from your sentences. Make sure, however, that you don't end up with a series of short, choppy sentences.

▶ Short, Choppy Sentences

Short sentences have their purpose. They tend to be clear and direct. A series of short sentences, however, can make the writing feel choppy and monotonous. There are many methods to revise short, choppy sentences, such as combining sentences (Lesson 4), or using *verbal phrases*. Verbal phrases are formed from verbs, but act like nouns, adjectives, or adverbs in a sentence. The most common verbal phrases are participial phrases, gerund phrases, infinitive phrases, and appositives.

► Participles and Participial Phrases

A participle is a verb form that can be used as an adjective, and a participial phrase is a phrase that contains a participle and any modifiers (Lesson 11). For example, when you change the verb "develop" to "developing" to describe something, you have created a participle. Adding modifiers to "developing" gives you a participial phrase.

Example
Developing off the coast of Haiti, a tropical storm brought rain and high winds to the West Indies.

The participial phrase *developing off the coast of Haiti* describes the tropical storm.

Example
We saw Lance Armstrong *receiving the yellow jersey* after the first mountain stage of the Tour de France.

The participial phrase *receiving the yellow jersey* describes Lance Armstrong.
Participial phrases can transform short, choppy sentences by adding description and detail.

► Gerunds and Gerund Phrases

Gerund phrases can also bring variety to your sentences. A gerund is a verb ending in -*ing* that serves as a noun.

Example
Running is a good way to stay in shape.
Running is formed from the verb *run* and is used as a noun in this sentence.

Example
Until I revise many times, I am not happy with my *writing*.
Writing is formed from the verb *write* and is used as a noun in this sentence.

Gerund phrases occur when a gerund is combined with modifiers.

Example
Working on the shrimp boat was a good summer job.
The phrase *working on the shrimp boat* serves as a noun in the sentence.

Example
My brother enjoys *skiing at Crystal Mountain*.
The phrase *skiing at Crystal Mountain* serves as a noun in the sentence.

► Infinitives and Infinitive Phrases

Infinitive phrases can also take the monotony out of your writing. An infinitive is a verb form composed of *to* plus the verb base.

Example
to walk   to speak   to cry   to leave   to eat
These verbs are often part of a verb chain, but are not the main action verb of the sentence.

Example
Fred tried *to speak* quickly.
The main verb is *tried*; what Fred *tried* is *to speak* quickly.

Example
There must be a way *to get past the road block*.

The infinitive phrase *to get past the road block* completes the phrase *must be a way*. The main verb in the sentence is *be*.

▶ Appositives and Appositive Phrases

Appositives add description and detail to your writing to make it clearer. An appositive is a noun or pronoun used to identify or explain another noun.

Example
My cousin *Alejandro* can play the piano.
   The noun *Alejandro* identifies the noun *cousin*, so it is an appositive.

   Appositives are also combined with modifiers to make appositive phrases.

Example
My grandmother, *a talented cook*, used to make an excellent pot roast.
   The phrase *a talented cook* is used to describe the noun *my grandmother*.

Exercise 3
Identify the italicized phrase in each of the following sentences as a participial phrase, a gerund phrase, an infinitive phrase, or an appositive phrase. Write the type of phrase on the lines provided. Answers can be found at the end of the lesson.

12. Steve Largent, *a former football player*, is now a politician.

_____

_____

13. The doctor will try *to diagnose* the illness.

_____

14. *Having scored the winning goal*, Christopher celebrated.

_____

_____

15. Mr. Ouimet enjoys *jogging to work*.

_____

16. *Invented for the U.S. military*, compact discs have many uses.

_____

_____

17. I can't find my shoes, *the ones with the red stripes*.

_____

_____

18. Vasili was glad *to be invited to the birthday party*.

_____

_____

▶ Punctuation

Punctuating sentences correctly helps you to avoid short, choppy sentences (Lessons 13, 14, and 15). Punctuation tells the reader how to read a sentence. If the reader can't get all the way through a sentence without stopping to take a breath, then the sentence is too long. On the other hand, if the sentence has too many places to pause, it will feel choppy. Commas tell the reader to pause, so using commas correctly and listening to the sound of your writing will help you to avoid creating choppy sentences.

Summary

In this lesson you have learned to revise awkward sentences using brief, concise language. You have learned to edit unnecessary and redundant words from longer sentences and to use verbal phrases to revise short, choppy sentences.

▶ Answers

Exercise 1

1. A fundamental part of cooking is making sure you have the right ingredients.
2. Every student deserves a fair chance to try out for intramural sports.
3. First, the Board of Directors cannot make a decision without a consensus.
4. Earlier today, my sister told me she would pick me up after work.
5. Various people in our office were in favor of moving the water cooler to a location that would be easier for everyone to reach.
6. One mistake some beginning swimmers make is forgetting to kick.

Exercise 2

7. More than any other invention, the telephone has changed the way we communicate.
8. The V-8 engine is powerful, but it isn't the only good engine design.
9. Several students fail, even though the curriculum is clear.
10. Scientists find it impossible to estimate the size of the universe, but they can come close.
11. The best skiers frequently suffer serious injuries.

Exercise 3

12. appositive
13. infinitive
14. participial
15. gerund
16. participial
17. appositive
18. infinitive

4 ▶ Creating Sentence Variety

LESSON SUMMARY

In this lesson, you will learn to revise your writing by combining sentences and by varying their length and type. The best writing uses a variety of sentence lengths and styles.

K eeping your reader involved can be an intricate dance with many different steps. Good writers fascinate their readers with the rhythm and flow of the language by using a combination of simple, compound, complex, and compound-complex sentences. Too many short, simple sentences in a row can blast from the page like the rat-a-tat-tat of a machine gun. Too many long, complex sentences take on the drone of a lazy summer afternoon. Just the right balance of each allows readers to follow with interest and attention.

Example 1

He woke up. He went downstairs. It was cold. The table was set. He sat down. Breakfast was hot. He ate quickly. He stood up. He cleaned his dishes. He went upstairs. He got dressed. It was time to start his day.

The example above shows how too many short sentences can make your writing sound choppy. The opposite happens when you use too many longer, more complex sentences in a row, as in Example 2 on the next page.

Example 2

As he always did, he woke up immediately and went down the steep staircase to the kitchen table. It was cold, but the table was set and breakfast was hot so he sat down and ate quickly. He stood up, cleaned his dishes, went upstairs, and got dressed; it was time to start his day.

Ideally, your writing should combine long and short sentences.

Exercise 1

On the lines below, rewrite the paragraph in Example 1 and 2 using a variety of long and short sentences. As you revise, it may be necessary to combine sentences. As discussed in the last chapter, combining a series of short, choppy sentences into one graceful sentence can transform an entire paragraph. One good sentence can express thoughts and ideas more clearly and succinctly than a couple of bad ones. A suggested answer is provided at the end of the lesson.

_____

_____

_____

_____

_____

_____

_____

▶ Conjunctions

Conjunctions are words that connect words, phrases, and clauses. The most common conjunctions are *and*, *but*, and *or*.

Example

Did you eat the last shrimp? Did you give it to someone else?

You is the subject of both sentences. Conjunctions can be used to eliminate repetition; in the example above, the combined sentence uses the subject only once.

Edited Example

Did you eat the last shrimp or give it to someone else?

In the example above, the part of the sentence after the conjunction, *give it to someone else,* is now a phrase. When you combine sentences using a conjunction, and the two sentences remain complete sentences after they have been combined, use a comma before the conjunction.

Edited Example

Did you eat the last shrimp, or did you give it to someone else?

Because the part of the sentence that follows the conjunction has both a subject and a predicate, it is an independent clause (also known as a complete sentence). Therefore, a comma appears before the conjunction.

Exercise 2

Circle the best conjunction to combine each sentence pair. Answers can be found at the end of the lesson.

1. Joe loves watching television. He hates soap operas.
   a. and
   b. but
   c. or

2. We can drive to San Francisco. We can take an airplane.
   a. and
   b. but
   c. or

3. The driver lost the map. The driver found the house anyway.
   a. and
   b. but
   c. or

4. The cowboys rounded up the cows. The cowboys put the cows in the corral.
   a. and
   b. but
   c. or

5. The carpenter built a chair. The carpenter built a footstool.
   a. and
   b. but
   c. or

▶ Overuse of Conjunctions

Conjunctions help us to combine sentences, but they can be overused, creating sentences that are too long.

Example
The drawbridge is raised, and the knights all take their positions along the battlement, and the king returns to the map room.

Edited Example
Raising the drawbridge, the knights all take their positions along the battlement while the king returns to the map room.

Another simple conjunction, *so*, is sometimes incorrectly used to begin sentences.

Example
So, the author used the literary technique of personification in her poem.

Edited Example
The author used the literary technique of personification in her poem.

So can be used to combine sentences, but it often sounds informal. You should be careful about using it too much in academic or formal writing. Generally, the proper way to use *so* is to combine it with *and* or *that* to form the phrases *and so* and *so that*.

Example
Rebecca wanted to improve her Spanish, so she moved to Mexico.

Edited Examples
Rebecca moved to Mexico because she wanted to improve her Spanish.
   Rebecca wanted to improve her Spanish, and so she moved to Mexico.

▶ Dividing Sentences

Long sentences connected by conjunctions can be revised by dividing them into two sentences. Remember, the goal is to use a variety of sentence lengths to give your writing an interesting rhythm and flow.

Example
I am a big tennis fan, and so I like to watch the matches on T.V. and sometimes I have a chance to see good tennis live and I try to get the best seats.

Edited Example
As a big tennis fan, I like to watch matches on T.V. When I have the chance to see good tennis live, I try to get the best seats.

Exercise 3
Revise the following sentences by using phrases and clauses to eliminate unnecessary conjunctions.

Write the new sentence on the lines. Answers can be found at the end of the lesson.

6. Our trip to Daniel's Seaside Resort took four hours, and the air conditioning did not work in the car, so we had to roll down the windows and a bee flew in.

_____

_____

_____

_____

7. The resort was smaller than we expected and more rustic, so we stayed in the main lodge most of the time and we played a lot of ping pong and we sat by the empty fireplace and talked.

_____

_____

_____

_____

8. We went outside and the sun burned my skin and the mosquitoes were everywhere, so we went back inside and we swam in the indoor pool and sat in the hot tub until our fingers were wrinkled.

_____

_____

_____

9. The game room had lots of video games and it had pinball and it had air hockey, so we took turns playing the games and watched while the others played.

_____

_____

_____

_____

10. Our summer trip ended too soon and we would like to go back and stay at the same place and in the same room next time, and we promise we will spend more time outside next year.

_____

_____

_____

_____

▶ Rearranging Sentences

Sometimes rearranging two short sentences can make one good sentence.

Example
The food is in the refrigerator. The food is from the Chinese restaurant.

Edited Example
The food from the Chinese restaurant is in the refrigerator.

In this example, the prepositional phrase *from the Chinese restaurant* is combined with the other sentence to make one sentence that is not choppy.

When combining sentences like this, you must occasionally add *-ing*, *-ed*, or *-ly* to one of the words.

Example
We saw a duck. The duck quacked at some geese.

Edited Example
We saw a duck quacking at some geese.

The rearranged words may need to be separated by a comma.

Example
Willie Mays hit many home runs in his career. Willie Mays was an outfielder.

Edited Example
Willie Mays, an outfielder, hit many home runs in his career.

You may have noticed that combined sentences often use *verbal phrases,* such as participial phrases, gerund phrases, infinitive phrases, and appositives as discussed in Lesson 3. Using these to combine two sentences can make for one graceful sentence. When they are used too much in one sentence, however, the sentence will be choppy.

Exercise 4

Combine the following sentences by rearranging them. Write the new sentence on the line. Answers can be found at the end of the lesson.

11. The garden is overgrown. The garden is at the back of the house.

_____

_____

12. Did you see that basketball player at the mall? The basketball player was tall.

_____

_____

13. I caught a frog. The frog hopped across the path.

_____

_____

14. Ace Green is a big donor to the public radio station. Ace Green is a local businessman.

_____

_____

▶ Varying Sentence Beginnings

Not only can you vary the length of your sentences, but you can vary the way they begin. This, too, will make your writing appeal to your reader. Normally, a simple sentence begins with the subject and ends with the predicate. It is very direct, which is good. Your reader won't get confused reading sentences in which you have directly linked the subject and predicate. However, a long run of these sentences may bore your reader.

Example
Ferns can add quality and texture to an ordinary garden. There are many different varieties. Ferns can be bought in nurseries or by mail order.

Edited Example
Ferns can add quality and texture to an ordinary garden. To order any number of varieties, visit your local nursery or peruse a mail order catalog.

► Single-Word Modifiers

Single-word modifiers used at the beginning of a sentence can help with variety and emphasis.

Example
Quite a few students have been taking performing arts classes recently.

Edited Example
Recently, quite a few students have been taking performing arts classes.

► Phrase Modifiers

Phrases can modify sentences and come at the beginning in place of the subject of the sentence for emphasis and variety.

Example
Joe lived in Chicago when he received his Master's degree and decided to become a teacher.

Edited Example
Living in Chicago, Joe received his Master's degree and decided to become a teacher.

In the above example, a *participial phrase*, as discussed in Lesson 3, begins the sentence.

Example
Wendy Nguyen wrote three different essays to win the prize.

Edited Example
To win the prize, Wendy Nguyen wrote three different essays.

In the above example, an *infinitive phrase* begins the sentence to offer variety.

Example
The shadows can frighten you in the woods.

Edited Example
In the woods, the shadows can frighten you.

In the above example, a *prepositional phrase* begins the sentence.

► Adverbial Phrases

An adverbial phrase is a prepositional phrase that modifies a verb, an adjective, or another adverb.

Examples of an adverbial phrase modifying a verb
Shara sings *in the shower*.

The prepositional phrase tells *where* she sings, so it is acting as an adverb.

Tom paints *with a fine brush*.

The prepositional phrase tells *how* he paints, so it is acting as an adverb.

Any time a prepositional phrase answers the questions *how, when, where, to what extent*, and *why*, it is an adverbial phrase.

Example of an adverbial phrase modifying an adjective
He is respectful *to his elders*.

The phrase *to his elders* modifies the adjective *respectful*.

Example of an adverbial phrase modifying an adverb
The ship listed far *to the starboard*.

The phrase *to the starboard* modifies the adverb *far*.

To offer variety, adverbial phrases can begin sentences.

Example
Before a race, Liam stretches.

▶ Clause Modifiers

Clauses can also be used at the beginning of a sentence.

Example
The roadie, when he heard the announcer introducing the band, worked quickly to tune the guitar.

Edited Example
When he heard the announcer introducing the band, the roadie worked quickly to tune the guitar.

Example
Detectives continue to search the crime scene for evidence because there have been no clues found so far.

Edited Example
Because there have been no clues found so far, detectives continue to search the crime scene for evidence.

Exercise 5

Circle the letter of the sentence in each group that begins with a single-word modifier, a phrase modifier, or a clause modifier and on the line provided, write the type of modifier that is used. Answers can be found at the end of the lesson.

15. a. In the boardroom, the discussion strayed from the planned agenda.
   b. Tarzan and Jane swung through the jungle.
   c. Many people do not believe in ghosts.

_____

16. a. A tornado set down in Oklahoma last month.
   b. The proud parents took pictures of their son.
   c. Lately, the weather has been warmer than usual this time of year.

_____

17. a. When the fifth-grader ate the sour candy, all of the first-graders watched.
   b. Oscar paid the rent.
   c. "Burnt Sienna" is my least favorite crayon color.

_____

18. a. Josh laughed at the sight of the miniature golf course.
   b. To sit through a long play can be difficult for a child.
   c. Yesterday was not my day.

_____

19. a. From that time on, the aqueducts brought water to Athens.
   b. Murphy's fish bait lures trout very well.
   c. The rose bush caught my pant leg.

_____

20. a. The telephone would not stop ringing.
   b. A crash course in sweeping would help Joan.
   c. Recently, my supervisor has been giving me more responsibility.

_____

21. a. The mountain slope looked like a challenge to climb.
   b. Because he ate too much pie, Sebastian had to lie down.
   c. The modern welfare state is a result of the Great Depression.

_____

If you know several different ways to begin sentences, you can choose when they are appropriate. Remember, the idea is to find a balance between being clear and being monotonous. Different sentence beginnings can help with both clarity and variety.

Summary

Varied writing will interest the reader. There are many ways to vary sentences, such as changing sentence length by combining shorter sentences and dividing longer sentences. Also, you can vary the way sentences begin by using different types of modifiers, such as single-word modifiers, phrase modifiers, and clause modifiers. Another strategy is to alternate long and short sentences.

▶ Answers

Exercise 1

The paragraph below is only a suggested answer. There are many ways to edit the paragraph using alternating long and short sentences.

Suggested Answer

He woke up immediately and went down the steep staircase to the kitchen table. It was cold. The table was set and breakfast was hot, so he sat down. He ate quickly. When he was finished, he stood up, cleaned his dishes, went upstairs, and got dressed. It was time to start his day.

Exercise 2

1. b. Joe loves watching television but hates soap operas.

2. c. We can drive to San Francisco or take an airplane.

3. b. The driver lost the map but found the house anyway.

4. a. The cowboys rounded up the cows and put them in the corral.

5. a. The carpenter built a chair and a footstool.

Exercise 3

6. Our trip in the car to Daniel's Seaside Resort took four hours, and the air conditioning did not work, so a bee flew in when we rolled down the windows.

7. The resort was smaller and more rustic than we expected, so we stayed in the main lodge most of the time, playing a lot of ping pong, sitting by the empty fireplace, and talking.

8. Outside, the sun burned my skin and the mosquitoes were everywhere, so we went back inside to swim in the indoor pool and sit in the hot tub until our fingers were wrinkled.

9. The game room had lots of video games, pinball and air hockey, so we took turns playing and watching while the others played.

10. Our summer trip ended too soon; we would like to go back and stay in the same room, and spend more time outside next year.

Exercise 4

11. The garden at the back of the house is overgrown.

12. Did you see that tall basketball player at the mall?

13. I caught a frog hopping across the path.

14. Ace Green, a local businessman, is a big donor to the public radio station.

Exercise 5

15. a. prepositional phrase

16. c. single-word modifier

17. a. clause modifier

18. b. phrase modifier

19. a. phrase modifier

20. c. single-word modifier

21. b. clause modifier

5 ▶ Shaping Paragraphs

LESSON SUMMARY

Good sentences need to be organized in strong, well-shaped paragraphs. A good paragraph contains a thesis sentence, supporting
sentences, and a concluding sentence. The average paragraph is four
to six sentences long. In this lesson you will learn to edit and revise
paragraphs to form a well-written composition.

A piece of writing is like a pearl necklace. One idea strings the whole piece together, but each
piece is slightly different. Paragraphs are the pearls. Each paragraph relates one topic that is
part of the whole thesis. Paragraphs exist together to form a coherent, well-conceived piece
of writing. Each paragraph—while it discusses a different subject from the others—follows more or less the
same structure.

A paragraph should begin with a thesis statement that presents the main idea of the paragraph. This
sentence is often referred to as the topic sentence. A good topic sentence clearly identifies the content of the
paragraph. The sentences that follow it develop the main idea, provide examples, quotes, and proof. A paragraph ends with a concluding statement that is also a transition to the next paragraph.

Some writers have difficulty determining where to put paragraph breaks. If you used a prewriting
activity, such as clustering or webbing, or started with an outline, it should help you determine how to group
information into paragraphs (Lesson 1). For example you can look at your cluster or word web for ideas that
have two or more parts or topics. In an outline, each heading (marked by a Roman numeral, for example)
typically signifies a new paragraph. If you are revising a piece of writing and you do not have any prewriting notes or outline, look for sentences that concern the same topic, and group them into paragraphs.

▶ Topic Sentences

A topic sentence has two purposes beyond identifying the main idea of the paragraph. It must present a statement that introduces all of the ideas contained within the paragraph, and the topic it introduces must be narrow enough to be completely developed in the paragraph. If the topic is too broad, you won't be able to discuss it completely in one paragraph. If it is too narrow, you will run out of ideas before you have a complete paragraph written.

The topic sentence must also grab the reader's attention. Like a headline in the newspaper, a topic sentence announces the main idea using language that will make the reader want to continue reading. This is also known as a "hook."

Topic Sentence as the First Sentence

The most common place to put the topic sentence is at the beginning of the paragraph. This gives the reader the clearest idea of what is going to be discussed in the paragraph. The topic sentence can go elsewhere in the paragraph, but if it is the first sentence, the reader will be prepared for what is to come.

Example
Computer programmers perform two main tasks when programming a computer. First, they must break down the instructions into clear, step-by-step tasks. Second, they must give directions in a computer-based language such as DOS. When these two tasks are completed properly, the computer will be able to do what the programmer has asked.

The topic sentence in this example is "Computer programmers perform two main tasks when programming a computer." This is the main idea of

the paragraph, and it is explained by the supporting sentences.

Topic Sentence in the Middle

While putting the topic sentence at the beginning of the sentence is the clearest way to write, it is not the only option. It can be placed in the middle of the paragraph, also.

Example
Who is the greatest cyclist of all time? Many people would choose Lance Armstrong. Lance Armstrong overcame cancer to win the grueling Tour de France multiple times. Diagnosed with testicular cancer that had spread to his lungs and brain, Lance underwent surgery and chemotherapy. He lost a significant amount of weight during his illness and was dropped by his cycling team. In a little over three years, however, he returned victorious to the Tour de France, becoming only the second American rider to win the coveted yellow jersey signifying the overall best time in the race.

In this example, the main idea of the paragraph is revealed in the third sentence, "Lance Armstrong overcame cancer to win the grueling Tour de France multiple times."

Topic Sentence at the End of the Paragraph

The topic sentence can be placed at the end of the paragraph. When it is at the end, it can effectively conclude the ideas that have led up to it.

Example
It is not a life of dinner parties and dancing. It is not an occupation that most practitioners find fun and light and easy. Writing is a solitary pursuit that most writers find repetitive and dull and the daily work a drudgery.

The topic of this short paragraph is, "Writing is a solitary pursuit that most writers find repetitive and dull and the daily work a drudgery." Placing it at the end of the sentence allows the reader to wonder what the paragraph is about and gives the topic sentence more impact.

In some cases, the topic sentence may be implied. This means that you can't locate it in a particular sentence, but the main idea is clearly developed enough in the paragraph that it is understood. Most often, this occurs in narrative writing, in which certain paragraphs may be devoted to describing a scene or explaining the plot of a story.

Exercise 1

Circle the letter of the topic sentence in each of the following paragraphs. Answers can be found at the end of the lesson.

1. **a.** He won Rookie of the year in 1947. **b.** He broke the color barrier in professional baseball. **c.** He excelled despite encountering racist players, managers, and fans and receiving death threats. **d.** Jackie Robinson single-handedly brought equality and civil rights to professional sports.

2. **a.** There are two primary approaches to learning a foreign language. **b.** First, there is the textbook approach of understanding the grammar and linguistics while studying vocabulary. **c.** Second, there is immersion in a foreign language, either in a school or in a foreign country where the language is spoken. **d.** Ideally, learning a foreign language involves a combination of both methods.

3. **a.** Did I come to Venice to see the beautiful St. Mark's Basilica? **b.** Am I here to walk across the elegant white stone Bridge of Sighs? **c.** The main reason I am in Venice is to learn to pilot

a gondola. **d.** A gondola is the traditional boat taxi of Venice's canals. **e.** It has a low hull and a steel prow and is rowed by a gondolier who wears an old-fashioned striped shirt and steers with a long oar.

▶ Topic Sentences in Persuasive Writing

The topic sentence often does not appear at the beginning of a sentence if the piece of writing is persuasive. Instead, the first sentence would be some kind of a lead sentence or a hook. It is always a good idea to capture your reader's attention as quickly as you can, but it is even more important to engage it immediately in a persuasive piece. Here are three recommended types of lead sentences.

Startling Statistic

If you can find a statistic about your topic that will make your readers interested right away, then you have a good lead. It is ineffective if you use a statistic that does not provoke them to think.

Example
In the roaring twenties, 30% of the money in the United States was controlled by 5% of the richest families.

Quote

For a persuasive piece about literature, or if you took good notes at a speech, for example, you can take a quote from your source and use it as your lead.

Example
The governor, in his speech about water rights, called the attempts to limit consumption "a waste of the taxpayers' time and effort."

Question

A rhetorical question is a question that does not necessarily need an answer, and is used by writers or speakers to persuade their audience to agree with an argument, or to raise a provocative issue. The answer to such a question is usually obvious and does not need to be stated, but you may choose to provide an answer at a later point in your paper. A question can be an effective way to start a paragraph, especially if it catches the reader's attention.

Example
Did the invention of barbed wire really change the pace of the westward movement?

If you are writing an academic paper, it is usually not acceptable to use the second person "you," as in "Have you ever wondered how many stars there are in the night sky?"

▶ Supporting Sentences

Since the topic sentence states the main idea of the paragraph, the supporting sentences must give enough information to develop that main idea clearly. A good, solid paragraph has at least two supporting details. A specific topic sentence serves to direct both the writer and the reader toward specific supporting details.

Example
There are different stances used when hitting a baseball (topic sentence). One stance involves keeping weight on the back foot and striding into the pitch. This swing is generally designed for power (supporting sentences developing the first idea). Another swing is called the "weight shift swing." Both of the batter's feet remain on the ground and the batter's weight shifts as the bat comes through the strike zone. This swing is

designed for contact hitters, as it tends to keep the bat level and allows the batter to hit to any field more easily (supporting sentences developing the second idea).

Some paragraphs are best developed using details from the five senses: taste, touch, sight, sound, and smell. These sensory details can support a topic sentence.

Example
The police arrived at the home of the alleged dog abuser. It smelled bad and the kennels were cold and dirty. The dogs were neglected.

Edited Example
The police arrived at the home of the alleged dog abuser and found the smell overwhelming. The dogs had not been let out of their kennels for days, and they had no clean place to lie down and no food or water. The generator used to heat the kennels emitted a piercing whine but no heat. Clearly, this was a case of animal neglect.

Facts, statistics, and specific examples can also be used to develop your paragraphs. When you revise, look for paragraphs that seem weak and lack solid evidence. You may have to do some more research to find information, but your paragraphs need to have enough information to deliver on their promise of supporting the topic sentence.

An anecdote or incident can tell a lot about a subject as well. An anecdote is a short story—often humorous—about an attention-grabbing event. Anecdotes can be very effective in making the reader visualize and identify with your main idea.

▶ Paragraph Organization

Once you have all your information for a paragraph, you must figure out how to organize it in a way that makes sense. There are several ways to organize information, such as *chronological order, order of importance, comparison/contrast, spatial order,* and *order of familiarity.*

Chronological Order

Chronos means time. Dividing the word *chronological* into two parts—*chrono* and *logical*—is a good way to remember that it means "logical time" order. Chronological order describes events in the order in which they took place. This is particularly effective for explaining a process. Perhaps you have to write an office memo explaining how the mail will be collected and delivered. Or maybe someone has borrowed your tent and needs directions from you for assembly. Step-by-step instruction is chronological order. Plot summaries for literature usually use chronological order. Used appropriately, chronological order adds to clarity.

Exercise 2

Rewrite the following sentences in the correct chronological order on the lines provided. Answers can be found at the end of the lesson.

4. Then you should find ways to speak to the students about the issues.

5. The results will be posted on the bulletin board in the main hall.

6. Finally, the students vote in the cafeteria.

7. The first step is to put up posters advertising your campaign for student body president.

8. The day before the election, you will speak at an assembly in the auditorium.

_____

_____

_____

_____

_____

If your paragraph gives information that makes sense in a chronological order, make sure it appears that way.

Order of Importance

One idea can have many aspects. If your topic sentence introduces an idea that can be supported by several details, you may want to present the supporting details in order of importance.

Example
Part-time jobs can be perfect for a student if they do not interfere with school. Most importantly, the employer must follow the state and federal regulations for employing minors. An employer should also offer flexibility with scheduling to accommodate major projects or extra-curricular activities for school. Some employers even offer incentive programs designed to encourage students to keep up their grades.

Compare and Contrast

To *compare* means to discuss the similarities between two or more things and to *contrast* means to discuss the differences between things. If your piece looks at two topics and the ways in which they are alike, you should use the comparison method of organizing your paragraph. If it examines differences, use the contrast method. If it looks at both similarities and differences, then you should consider organizing your paper so that you discuss similarities in one paragraph or group of paragraphs and differences in another. That way, the comparison is very clear for your reader.

Example

The San Juan Islands off the coast of Washington State and Cape Cod in Massachusetts are alike in many ways, but they are also different. Both areas are in coastal climates and have similar weather patterns. Both offer a similar, low-key lifestyle to the residents. Both are surrounded by natural beauty. The fish that provide a living to the local fishing population, however, differ considerably. The other wildlife, like birds and rodents, are also different. Finally, Cape Cod enjoys beautiful sunrises, while the sun sets over the ocean in the San Juan Islands, making the evening the most colorful time of the day.

Spatial Order

Spatial order means order in space. For example, if you wanted to describe to someone where your seats are for the concert, you might start with a seat number, then a row, then the section. You might have to expand further out into space by telling them what side of the stage you will sit on and how far back your seat is. This is spatial order.

Example

From the observation deck of the Empire State Building, one can see Central Park to the north. To the south are lower Manhattan, SoHo, and the financial district. One can see the the Statue of Liberty and the beautiful New York Harbor.

Order of Familiarity

If you are writing about a well-known topic, you might choose to organize your information into the order of familiarity. Start with the most commonly known information and move to information your reader may not know, or write it the other way around. Whether you go from the familiar to the unknown or the unknown to the familiar, you are organizing your information in order of importance.

Example

The Human Genome Project's goal is to define all human genes. Scientists have already described, in detail, the genes of simple species such as yeast, bacteria, roundworms, and fruit flies. Recently, they began to unlock the genomes of the cow, rat, and dog. What many people do not know is that scientists have been decoding the genes of the common house cat and finding similarities to human genes. The study shows that humans are more closely related to cats than to any other animal group studied so far except primates.

Different types of writing call for different organizational methods. Expository, persuasive, narrative, and descriptive writing all follow different patterns, and the way you organize each paragraph in each type of writing affects how the piece works as a whole. You must look at the purpose of your piece to determine the best way to organize it. Often, this kind of organization occurs during revision.

▶ Expository Writing

If your paragraph explains something or presents information, it is an expository paragraph. If it explains a process, it usually does so in chronological order. Transitional words such as *first, next*, and *finally* make the order clear. Paragraphs that define are also expository paragraphs. In this type of paragraph, your topic sentence would place the topic in a general category and then provide supporting details that describe specific characteristics to the reader. In this way, you narrow down your topic and clarify the way the topic differs from other topics.

Paragraphs that give reasons are also expository paragraphs. This kind of paragraph supports the main idea with facts. It may explain that something is true because of certain facts, or it may explain that an action or opinion is right because the facts support it. The most common way to organize this type of paragraph is using the order of importance method.

▶ Persuasive Writing

Persuasive writing is expository because it gives facts, but it also presents an opinion. There are many ways to organize persuasive writing. One common way is to present possible arguments against your opinion and show why these arguments are weak; then give the arguments in your favor. Another way is to state an opinion and then give evidence to support it. A persuasive technique gives your supporting information in order of importance, with the last fact or statistic being the strongest or most effective reason.

▶ Narrative Writing

Narrative writing tells a story. The structure and methods for organizing narrative writing are different from expository writing because narrative writing has a different purpose. Simple narratives describe the events that happened, usually in chronological order. Complex narratives focus on the resolution of a conflict and usually have a theme, characters, setting, and other elements of a short story.

▶ Descriptive Writing

Using words to create a picture is called descriptive writing, which uses sensory details to establish a mood and point of view. Descriptive paragraphs often contain many adjectives to describe the subject at hand clearly. Descriptive writing can stand alone as a descriptive piece, or it can be included as part of a narrative. Regardless, it should be organized into a well-shaped paragraph.

▶ Transitional Concluding Sentences

Well-shaped paragraphs have the same components as a well-shaped composition: a beginning, middle, and end. Once you have a topic sentence and some supporting sentences, it is time to end the paragraph. Concluding sentences are a form of transition. Moving smoothly from one paragraph to the other requires transitions (Lesson 6). Transitional concluding sentences sum up what has come before, and can be used in any paragraph.

Because paragraphs themselves mirror the structure of an essay, the longer the paragraph, the more likely it will need some kind of summing up. The concluding sentence might restate an idea expressed in the paragraph's topic sentence, summarize the main points, or add a comment to the ideas expressed in the paragraph. When revising, it is up to you to decide if a paragraph needs a concluding sentence, but a general rule would be to use them only with paragraphs that have many supporting details.

Always avoid weak concluding sentences like, "Now I have given four reasons why Italian food is better than Mexican food." The idea of a concluding sentence is not to tell what you just wrote, but to wrap up the subject. In general, you should avoid talking directly to the reader in academic essays because it is considered by many to be too familiar. In business writing, it depends on your audience, but it is better to be overly formal than overly familiar at any time.

Summary

This lesson has shown you how to combine sentences together into strong, well-shaped paragraphs. You have learned what a thesis sentence is, what support your thesis statement needs, and how to write concluding sentences. When you revise your own writing, you should now be able to make good decisions about the shape and organization of your paragraphs.

▶ Answers

Exercise 1
1. d.
2. a.
3. c.

Exercise 2
The day before the election, you will speak at an assembly in the auditorium. The first step is to put up posters advertising your campaign for student body president. Then you should find ways to speak to the students about the issues. Finally, the students vote in the cafeteria. The results will be posted on the bulletin board in the main hall.

6 ▶ Using Transitions

LESSON SUMMARY

The word "transition" means to pass from one to another. This lesson will show you different ways to use transitional words and phrases to unify a piece of writing.

Imagine you are playing music at a dance party. Your goal is to keep the dance floor filled with happy people. To do this, you must keep the beat and the energy going from one song to the next, because people often decide to sit down when there is an awkward break between songs. If you make a smooth transition, the dancing never stops.

When writing an essay, transitions are just as important. You are trying to keep your reader reading, and that means making smooth transitions between words and ideas within sentences, between sentences, and between paragraphs.

▶ Linking Expressions

Linking expressions help your writing flow. Following is a list of words and phrases that serve as transitions.

therefore	furthermore
consequently	however
accordingly	as a result
an example of this	similarly
finally	besides
lastly	nevertheless
also	on the contrary
meanwhile	on the other hand
soon	after all
in other words	such
in addition	likewise
then again	as might be expected

▶ Transitions Within a Sentence

Linking expressions can be used within a sentence to connect two related clauses.

Example
To plant similar trees, *on the other hand,* could result in one disease wiping out all the trees on the block.

If used to connect two sentences, transition words will appear at the beginning of the second sentence.

Example
Skateboarding is prohibited in certain public areas. *As a result,* many skaters use designated skating areas and are working hard to convince the city council to build more skate parks.

A strategy for revising your writing to clarify and reinforce the connections between ideas is to closely examine the transitions between sentences. As always, it is helpful if your draft is double-spaced. First, draw a box around the last word of the first sentence and the first word of the next sentence. Identify the relationship that connects the sentences. If the relationship is clear, then move on the next sentence. If the relationship is unclear, and you cannot identify it, try adding a linking expression to serve as a transition.

Exercise 1
Revise the following sentences by writing a linking expression on the line provided. Your answers will vary depending on your word choice, but suggested answers can be found at the end of the lesson.

1. We wanted to go to a movie, _____ the theater was closed.

2. Joey's car was full of gas, _____ we drove it to the beach.

3. The ballet did not impress the students. _____, the break dancers were a big hit.

4. We visited Phoenix, Tucson, Albuquerque, Santa Fe, and _____, Las Vegas.

5. Some chili recipes do not include kidney beans. _____ would be the traditional West Texas chili.

The purpose of using transitions between sentences is to create unified paragraphs. Like the rungs of a ladder, unified paragraphs allow the reader to move one step at a time and to follow the main idea to its conclusion.

▶ Transitions Between Paragraphs

As discussed in Lesson 5, paragraphs are organized in many ways. The same transitions—or linking expressions—used to connect sentences can be used to connect paragraphs, and will help clarify the relationship between ideas in paragraphs.

Checking to see that your transitions between paragraphs are clear is similar to the method you used when checking transitions between sentences. Place a box around the last sentence of a paragraph and the first sentence of the next paragraph. Identify the relationship that connects the two ideas. If the relationship is clear and the transition is smooth, then there is no need to revise. If the relationship is not clear and there is not a smooth transition, sentences within the paragraphs may need to be rearranged, the paragraphs may need to be better organized, or the transition between the paragraphs may need to be revised. Transitions between paragraphs are very important for maintaining coherence.

Chronological Order

Chronological order is shown by using such transition words as *first, second, finally, next, then, afterward, later, before, eventually,* and *in the future.*

Example
<u>Before</u> the employees arrive in the morning, the building is empty. It is <u>then</u> that the janitor can clean thoroughly.

Example
<u>First</u>, it is necessary to collect sources about your research topic. <u>Second</u>, you must put these sources in order of importance. <u>Finally</u>, you must read the information and take notes.

Chronological order is a common organizational technique for writers of fiction, as you will see in the next example.

Example
"In consideration of the day and hour of my birth, it was declared by the nurse, and by some sage women in the neighbourhood who had taken a lively interest in me several months before there was any possibility of us becoming personally acquainted, first, that I was destined to be unlucky in life; and secondly, that I was privileged to see ghosts and spirits; both these gifts inevitably attaching, as they believed, to all unlucky infants of either gender, born towards the small hours on a Friday night."

—*David Copperfield*

Spatial Order

Transition words that show spatial order are *beside, in the middle, next to, to the right, on top of, in front of, behind, against,* and *beneath.* Spatial order is helpful when describing a place or the setting of a story.

Example
Against the wall, there is a dresser. *On top* of the dresser is where Brad keeps his spare change.

Example
There is a damp cave *beneath* the house. If you enter the cave, take the fork *to the right*, or, as legend has it, you might disturb the ancient spirits.

Order of Importance

Transition words that show the order of importance are *more, less, most, least, most important, least important,* and *more importantly.*

Example
Yesterday was a beautiful, sunny day, but *more importantly*, it was my birthday.

Comparison and Contrast

Transition words that show comparison and contrast are *likewise, however, similarly, in contrast, a different kind, unlike this,* and *another difference.*

Example
The book *Of Mice and Men* begins with George and Lennie walking through the woods. *In*

contrast, the movie begins with a woman in a red dress running through a field.

Example

My mother and grandmother both taught pre-school. I chose, *however*, to become an engineer.

Cause and Effect

Transition words used to show cause and effect are *therefore*, *as a result of*, *consequently*, *thus*, *one cause*, *one effect*, *another cause*, and *another effect*.

Example

Security officers guarded the gates of the airport. *As a result*, traffic slowed considerably on the highway.

Example

The recipe calls for two tablespoons of butter, and, *consequently*, the cookies will be thin and crisp.

Classification

Transition words that show classification are helpful, especially in scientific writing where classification is an important step in understanding the natural world. Transition words include *another group*, *the first type*, *one kind*, *other sorts*, *other types*, and *other kinds*.

Example

One type of tennis player, like John McEnroe, lets his emotions show on the court. *Another type* of player stays calm throughout the match, whether the calls are bothersome or not.

▶ Introducing Examples

To introduce examples in your piece of writing, you can use transition words such as *for example*, *one example*, *one kind*, *one type*, *one sort*, and *for instance*.

Example

One example of a Greek tragedy is *Antigone*.

Example

Most insects have very short life spans. *For instance*, the fruit fly can expect to complete its life cycle in less than 48 hours.

▶ Introducing Contradictions

When comparing and contrasting in a piece of writing, you often must introduce contradictions. They can be very effective tools for persuasion. Transition words that introduce contradictions are *nonetheless*, *however*, *in spite of*, *otherwise*, *instead*, and *on the contrary*.

Example

The storm continued to toss the ship and managed to snap off the tip of the mast. *In spite of* this, they sailed on, desperate to reach Hawaii.

Example

Growers have recently marketed prunes as dried plums. *Nonetheless*, most people still refer to them as prunes.

▶ Introducing Conclusions, Summaries, or Generalizations

Wrapping up your piece is a form of transition. As you conclude your work, you need to lead your reader to the end. Transition words for concluding are *in conclusion*, *therefore*, and *as a result*. Summaries and generalizations can be effectively introduced using *in summary* or *in general*.

Example
Therefore, Cinco de Mayo is celebrated differently in the United States than in Mexico.

Example
In general, the phenomenon of the Bermuda Triangle is believed to be coincidental.

Exercise 2

Revise the sentences below by following the directions in parentheses. Write the new sentences on the lines. Suggested answers can be found at the end of the lesson.

6. It rained all morning. We went to the park. (Begin the second sentence with a transition word that introduces **contradiction**.)

_____

_____

7. The company wants to hire experienced employees. Those people with no experience need not apply. (Combine these sentences using a **cause and effect** transition word.)

_____

_____

8. Sylvia greeted all of her guests at the door. She seated them at the dinner table. (Combine these sentences using a transition word that shows **chronological order**.)

_____

_____

9. Bob Marley used Sly and Robbie for a rhythm section. Peter Tosh recorded with Sly and Robbie on at least one of his records. (Begin the second sentence with a transition word that shows **comparison and contrast**.)

_____

_____

10. We kept adding water to the paint. It was too thin to use. (Begin the second sentence with a transition word used for **concluding**.)

_____

_____

▶ Pronouns as Linking Words

Parts of a paragraph can be linked in other ways besides using traditional transition words. Pronouns link words and sentences when they refer to a noun or another pronoun from a previous sentence.

Example
John left work early to go to a doctor's appointment. *He* is getting *his* annual physical.

The pronouns *he* and *his* refer to the noun *John* from the first sentence. Without the first sentence, the reader would not know who *he* is. Therefore, the sentences are linked together by a pronoun.

Pronouns can link entire pieces of writing together. Make sure, however, that if you use pronouns frequently in a piece of writing, they clearly refer to their antecedents. A string of unclear or ambiguous pronouns will confuse the reader.

▶ Nouns as Linking Words

Nouns can serve as linking words when repeated from one sentence to another.

Example

The people of Philadelphia have great *pride* in their city. This *pride* comes from Philadelphia's long and glorious history as one of the seats of democracy in the United States.

Example

Everyone is very *excited* about our long weekend in the Poconos. Our *excitement* increased when the weather report called for snow.

► Rephrasing as a Method of Linking

Words and ideas can also be rephrased and used again, as in the following sentences.

Example

Everyone in the band looks forward to the *State Jazz Band Finals*. This *annual conference* provides an opportunity for young musicians from all over California to play and listen to jazz together.

► Linking Paragraphs

Repeating or rephrasing nouns and pronouns not only links sentences, but can be used to create transitions between paragraphs as well. To make a transition between paragraphs clear, follow the methods described above, making sure to repeat or rephrase the words from the last sentence of one paragraph in the first sentence of the next. This can successfully bridge the two paragraphs and connect ideas.

Example

Black bears consistently cause problems for companies that remove trash in Colorado. They break into both residential and commercial trash containers, leaving behind a mess and causing bears and humans to come into ever closer contact.

This issue prompted the development of bear-proof trash containers. They have a self-locking lid that is heavy enough to close on its own, and can be bolted to a cement pad.

Summary

When revising your writing, examine your transitions between sentences and between paragraphs. If they do not effectively move your idea along, or are not smooth, use the methods and strategies you have learned in this lesson to improve them.

► Answers

Exercise 1

Remember, these are suggested answers. Other transition words could work if the sentence makes sense with them.

1. however
2. therefore
3. on the other hand
4. lastly
5. an example of this

Exercise 2

Again, these are suggested answers.

6. It rained all morning. In spite of this, we went to the park.
7. The company wants to hire experienced employees, therefore, those people with no experience need not apply.
8. Sylvia greeted all of her guests at the door, then she seated them at the dinner table.
9. Bob Marley used Sly and Robbie for a rhythm section. Likewise, Peter Tosh recorded with Sly and Robbie on at least one of his records.
10. We kept adding water to the paint. As a result, it was too thin to use.

7 ▶ Establishing a Writing Style

LESSON SUMMARY

This lesson will help you develop your style through revision to make your writing suit any occasion. It discusses the elements of style, including tone, voice, audience, and purpose.

A version of the golden rule applies to writing: write how you would like to read. There's a reason you like to read certain articles, magazines, and books, and it is not just because of the content. For example, if you read the sports section of the newspaper often enough, you may find that you like the articles by a certain reporter better than the others. Perhaps you have read everything one novelist has written, regardless of the subject matter, because you like the way he or she writes. What you appreciate is the author's tone, voice, and style.

▶ Tone

When you speak, you use a certain tone of voice. Writing has a tone, also. For instance, if your piece is a narrative essay about a time in your life when you were treated unfairly, you might decide that a direct tone is the best approach. Tone is dictated by the audience and purpose of the piece. Good writers use a tone that will not put off their readers and that suits their writing. While the tone can be revised, the audience and purpose should be determined before you begin to write.

Example

I will take action the next time I see a person treat another human being differently because of the color of his or her skin. I will speak up, loud and clear, and make my voice heard by not only those around me, but by all the creatures of the earth. I will not stand by and let injustice happen.

▶ Audience

The audience of a piece is the intended reader. Who do you expect to read your essay or memo? For example, the tone would be different in a letter to a prospective employer than in a note to a friend. That is because the audience is different. In both of those cases, the audience is one person. When something is published or shared, such as a letter to the editor or a newsletter, the audience is broader, and you should be careful that the language doesn't alienate or offend your readers. Keep your audience in mind as you write and revise to ensure that you are using language appropriate for that particular audience.

▶ Purpose

What is the objective of the piece? Are you writing to persuade someone to agree with you? Are you writing to amuse the reader with a funny story? Are you writing to share information? You must know the purpose of the piece before you write, and you will be sure to meet your goal.

If you offend your audience, you will not achieve your purpose. For example, if you are writing a persuasive piece and your reader feels you are being condescending, he or she may stop reading.

Persuasive Example

I am not sure you would be able to understand how important the governor's race is, but I will try to explain because I want you to vote for Larry Kaley.

This example makes it sound like the reader couldn't possibly be smart enough to understand a political concept, and its tone is arrogant. This approach does not achieve its purpose but could be revised to be more appealing to a voter.

Edited Example

The choice of a governor for our state relies on every voter. The two candidates who are running are excellent, but Larry Kaley is the better choice for many reasons.

When writing to inform, also known as *expository writing,* your purpose is to present information and facts in an objective manner, without persuasion or opinion. Note the difference in the way a topic is introduced in the following examples.

Expository Example

The 1999 U.S. Women's World Cup sold over 650,000 tickets.

Persuasive Example

The U.S. Women's World Cup soccer team is the best in the world.

Exercise 1

Read the topics in this exercise and circle the letter that identifies the type of writing needed for each topic. Answers can be found at the end of the lesson.

1. the need to arrive on time
   a. persuasive
   b. expository

2. Ancient Greek pottery
   a. persuasive
   b. expository

3. reasons to quit smoking
   a. persuasive
   b. expository

4. the history of tobacco
   a. persuasive
   b. expository

5. why lacrosse is America's game
   a. persuasive
   b. expository

▶ Voice

Most successful writers have the ability to adjust their voice to fit the occasion. Adding facts and statistics, sensory details, examples, anecdotes, quotations, or definitions to your piece can change the voice.

▶ Authoritative Voice

An expository piece of writing can include facts and statistics that give the voice an authoritative tone, the tone of an expert in the field. A fact is a provable truth. A statistic is data, usually numerical, that describes a fact. Statistics add an element of authority to an expository piece.

Example without facts
Solar eclipses occur fairly often. People should not be afraid of disasters happening because of an eclipse.

Example with facts
Solar eclipses occur approximately once every hundred years. In fact, the moon blocked our view of the sun twice in the twentieth century. There is no reason to be afraid an eclipse will cause a disaster because during the course of human history, we have survived at least fifty such alignments.

Example without statistics
In general, young Americans watch a lot of television. Some children spend almost all their time watching TV.

Example with statistics
Studies have shown that the average American child spends three to four hours a day watching television, which adds up to 1,500 hours per year, compared to 900 hours spent in the classroom.

To sound like an expert, you must conduct research. When you come across an interesting fact or statistic, make a note of it so you can add it to your piece during revision. (When you make notes, don't forget to write the page number and source as well. You will need to cite the source of this information in your writing. See pages 67–68 for more about this.) Facts and statistics not only support your thesis in an expository essay, but they can also be a very effective way to begin a persuasive piece.

You must carefully distinguish between facts and opinions. An opinion states a judgment or a belief and cannot necessarily be proved. In all communication, you must be able to tell the difference between facts and opinions, whether in an advertisement, political campaign, newspaper, or when discussing automotive repairs with your mechanic.

Example of fact
Three hundred people attended the amateur dog show.

Example of opinion
Many people attended the amateur dog show.

Example of fact
The average work week in the United States consists of five eight-hour days.

Example of opinion
The average work week in the United States is too long.

Opinions often use words like *most, should, should not, greatest, best, worst,* and *least.* When you include a fact about one thing and apply it to all similar things, you are making a generality. Generalities express opinions also, so be careful when using words like *all, none,* and *every* in expository writing.

Exercise 2

Identify the following sentences as fact or opinion by circling the correct answer. Answers can be found at the end of the lesson.

6. Stephen King is the greatest writer today.
   a. fact
   b. opinion

7. The number of camping permits issued in Yellowstone National Park rose by 12% this year.
   a. fact
   b. opinion

8. Every 16 year old should be allowed to drive a car.
   a. fact
   b. opinion

9. People who do not take care of their pets are the worst.
   a. fact
   b. opinion

10. Biographies, autobiographies, and popular histories are examples of non-fiction.
   a. fact
   b. opinion

When you can discern facts from opinions and apply them appropriately, your persuasive and expository writing will be more effective.

▶ Sensory Details

Sensory details are necessary to give a reader a thorough explanation. Think about the five senses (taste, touch, sight, smell, and hearing) as you revise your writing. If you see a place where a sensory detail would make a difference or improve your piece, add the description during the revision process. Keep in mind, however, that many sensory details involve opinion, and those that do are not appropriate in an expository piece. In descriptive, narrative, and persuasive pieces, however, sensory details can help you achieve your purpose with style.

Example without sensory detail
Lightning hit the barn and caused damage.

Example with sensory details
A jagged lightning bolt pierced the barn, noisily splitting it in two and filling the air with the smell of sulfur.

Example without sensory detail
The chocolate cake tasted great.

Example with sensory detail
As my fork cut through the dark chocolate cake, the warm fudge middle oozed out, mingling its scent with the vanilla ice cream and forming a swirling lake around the strawberry garnish.

When revising descriptive writing, follow these basic rules:

- Think about the focus of each paragraph.
- Clearly identify the person or object you are describing.
- Include concrete details along with sensory details.
- Appeal to a variety of senses, not just sight.
- Arrange the sensory details logically.

▶ Examples and Definitions

Upon reading your draft, if you find any place where your point is unclear, try adding an example. Transition words such as *for example* and *for instance* can introduce an example, but not every example has to begin with those words.

Example
Biely had a hard time hitting off of left-handed pitchers. For example, when the left-handed Jones pitched, Biely went 0 for 6.

Example
Wally liked to outdo the other kids on Halloween. He would spend weeks working on his costume and comb thrift stores for accessories. On the big night, while other kids walked door to door with small plastic pumpkins for their candy, Wally would ride his scooter to get to more houses. He even carried a pillow case to hold all his loot.

How did Wally like to outdo the other kids? The examples show that he would spend weeks on his costume, ride his scooter, and carry a pillow case to hold more candy. These examples clearly illustrate the thesis sentence.

Definitions can help your reader understand—especially if you are using unfamiliar language, such as jargon or foreign words—or describing a place.

Example
Mike studied HTML, a computer language used to make websites interactive.

Without the definition, those readers who are unfamiliar with basic website design would be confused.

Example
She made up the word "brujoron" to describe a cartoon character she didn't like. It combines the Spanish word for witch with the English word "moron."

Example
Penny rode her bike over the St. John's Bridge, the southernmost bridge within the city limits.

▶ Quotations

Quotations are an excellent way to support your thesis, especially if you are writing about history or literature. One common misconception is the belief that you can only quote words from your research if they already appear in quotation marks, such as dialogue. This is not the case. Any words you find in your sources that you feel would strengthen your argument can be quoted. If you use quotation marks, make sure the words that appear in quotes are *verbatim*—Latin for "word for word." These are called direct quotes.

Example of a source
In his theory of relativity, Einstein explained that motion and time are relative to the observer. As an explanation of his theory, he said to imagine that you are traveling on a train at 50 miles per hour

and you throw a ball out the window at 10 miles per hour. To you, the ball is traveling at 10 miles per hour, but to an observer standing beside the train tracks, the ball is traveling at 60 miles per hour. The measurement is relative to the observer.

Example of a direct quote
Einstein had many ways of describing his theories. He used an anecdote about a train to show that "the measurement is relative to the observer."

An indirect quote is when you use someone else's words, but not exactly word for word. Indirect quotes do not need quotation marks.

Example of an indirect quote
Einstein said motion and time are relative.

If you use someone else's words or ideas and do not give them credit, it is called *plagiarism* and is the intellectual equivalent of stealing. Make sure that when you quote someone, you place their last name, and the page number where you found the information in parentheses at the end of your sentence. If you are using more than one work by the same writer, include the title of the work you are citing in the parentheses. Be sure to provide your reader with a full list of works you have cited at the end of your paper. Consult a style manual for the proper methods of citing sources in Appendix B.

If your goal is to make your writing clear, examples, definitions, and quotations can help.

▶ Anecdotes

Anecdotes are brief stories used to illustrate a point. They can serve as examples and can make your writing more interesting and descriptive

Example without anecdote
The early homesteaders in eastern Washington State did whatever it took to increase their land holdings.

Example with anecdote
The early homesteaders in eastern Washington State did whatever it took to increase their land holdings. As a teenager, my great grandfather Ray worked for a homesteader. He recalls a land auction that took place on a piece of flat, isolated land that was for sale. An unknown city dweller intended to bid on the land, but instead of riding out to the auction, he had telephone poles installed every 100 feet to carry a direct line to the auctioneer. As the auction progressed, Ray's boss grew tired of being outbidded, so he sent my great grandfather off with an ax and the instructions to ride his horse a ways out and chop down one of the poles. He did just that, and remembers the sound of the telephone line snapping and the sight of pole after pole toppling like dominoes off into the horizon.

When reading over your draft, mark any places where examples, anecdotes, or quotations could make the description more powerful and then add them as you revise your writing. For some audiences, it is appropriate to use informal language, as in the above anecdote. Terms like *city dweller* and *ride his horse out a ways* suit the language of the piece. You can make this decision by knowing your audience.

▶ Informal Language

Informal language gives your writing an informal tone. One way to think of informal language is that it resembles the way we speak. When we write in the same way that we speak, we tend to use slang, colloquialisms, and contractions. If your audience is a good friend, then an informal tone is most likely what you would use when writing to him or her.

▶ Slang

Slang is language that is particular to a group. If you include slang in your writing, those readers who are not a part of that group may not be familiar with or understand the words you use. It is very possible that those readers may lose interest.

Examples
The judge sentenced the robber to six years in the *slammer.*

Do you have a DVD player at your *crib*?

▶ Colloquial Language

Colloquial comes from a Latin word meaning *to speak together.* Colloquialisms are similar to slang, except they are more widely understood, and they are usually sayings. Colloquialisms are used widely, and because of that, they can be stale. Revise them out of your writing when possible. Replace a trite phrase with figurative language that expresses the same idea, but in a fresh way.

Examples
She arrived late to work because she was *dragging her heels.*

I knew I was a *goner* as soon as I saw James on the mound.

Edited Examples
Procrastination was her worst habit, and as a result she arrived late to work everyday.

James was an all-star pitcher, and I knew that I would hear the umpire calling, "Strike three," in just a few minutes.

▶ Figurative Language

Figurative language includes all the writing techniques that help your words paint a picture. Good descriptive writing encourages the reader to form mental images of what is being described, and figurative language can be a powerful tool. Two common types are metaphor and simile. Both of these involve comparing two unlike things. The difference is that a simile uses "like" or "as" in its comparison.

Example of metaphor
When the smell hits me, I am a shark, slicing between the people on the sidewalk and attacking the hot dog stand.

Example of simile
When the smell hits me, I am like a shark, slicing between the people on the sidewalk and attacking the hot dog stand.

A good metaphor or simile in place of an overused phrase can make your writing come alive.

Example using colloquialism
I am dog tired.

Example using simile
I am as tired as a cat in the dog pound.

▶ Contractions

Another casual form that can be easily revised out of your writing is the use of contractions. Contractions shorten word pairs by using an apostrophe.

Example
He *doesn't* think *they're* coming.

Some common contractions use the apostrophe in place of the "o" in "not," such as *didn't, doesn't, shouldn't, hasn't, aren't, wouldn't, haven't,* or *isn't.* Some use an apostrophe in place of the "i" in "is," such as *it's, there's, he's,* and *she's,* or the "a" in "are," such as *we're,* and *they're.*

Not only do contractions present an opportunity to make errors in punctuation, but they are informal and are sometimes considered "lazy writing."

Exercise 3

In the sentence pairs below, circle the letter of the sentence that uses informal language. Answers can be found at the end of the lesson.

11. a. The leaves of the trees turned brilliant orange and red in the fall.
   b. The leaves of the trees were way orange and red in the fall.

12. a. He didn't have the keys to the car.
   b. He did not have the keys to the car.

13. a. Outside, it was raining very hard.
   b. Outside, it was raining cats and dogs.

14. a. My mom was mad that Christine was totally late for dinner.
   b. My mom was angry that Christine was late for dinner.

15. a. George sold his business lock, stock, and barrel.
   b. George sold his entire business.

When you are writing dialogue in a story, informal language can be appropriate. In fact, the way characters speak reveals quite a bit about who

they are. Language that is so informal that it sounds uneducated makes it seem as if the speaker has not learned proper English. Some contractions that fall into this category would be *here're, ain't, them's, shouldn't've, di'n't, they's, his'n,* and *there've.*

Example
Harry looked at the pile of debris and said, "*them's* the breaks."

Example
"I *ain't never gonna* get to get to ride on *a* airplane," Fran whined.

These examples combine forms of informal language such as contractions, colloquialisms, and improper usage. Other forms of informal language involve improper agreement (Lessons 9, 10, and 19). While it is true that we use informal language every day in our speech, it should be judiciously used in writing.

▶ Formal Language

Formal language, unlike informal language, uses no slang words, colloquialisms, or contractions. When you are not sure exactly who your audience is, it is safest to use formal language. Formal language will not offend anyone because it is not disrespectful, and it will not alienate anyone who does not understand certain slang or colloquialisms. Formal language tends to use more long and complex sentence structures and vocabulary that is more accurate and specific. Very formal language, such as for ceremonies, often uses archaic words, or old words no longer in common usage, to add dignity to solemn occasions. Ceremonies that quote from ancient texts like the Bible are a good example of this, because ancient texts contain words that are no longer in common usage. However, you should be careful not to use such formal language that your reader doesn't understand what you are trying to say.

Exercise 4

Circle the letter for the appropriate language to use for each of the following situations. Answers can be found at the end of the lesson.

16. a letter to the editor
   a. formal
   b. informal

17. a letter to a friend
   a. formal
   b. informal

18. a cover letter to a prospective employer
   a. formal
   b. informal

19. a wedding ceremony
   a. formal
   b. informal

20. a love letter
   a. formal
   b. informal

▶ Point of View

The first-person point of view is used when the writer is referring to himself or herself as "I" in the writing. First-person pronouns include *I, we, me, us, my, myself* and *our.*

Example
When I arrive in a foreign country, I spend time orienting myself with a map and making plans to see certain sights that I think will be interesting.

The first-person point of view brings the reader and writer closer together, while the third-person point of view separates them with a formal distance. Third-person pronouns are *she, he, one, they, her, him, them, hers, his,* and *theirs.*

Example
When tourists arrive in a foreign country, they should spend some time orienting themselves with a map and making plans to see certain sights they think will be interesting.

The second example sentence above is more formal sounding, even though the subject is the same. Third-person point of view has a distance that we associate with formality. Using the third-person pronoun "one" sounds even more formal.

Example
When one arrives in a foreign country, one should spend some time orienting oneself with a map and making plans to see certain sights one thinks will be interesting.

The second-person point of view uses *you* and *your.* Directly addressing the reader, in the second-person point of view, is considered informal.

The point of view you choose for your piece should remain consistent throughout. Switching from first-person to third-person point of view can confuse the reader.

Inconsistent example
I had a great trip to Chicago. You could see the Sears Tower and Wrigley Field.

Edited example
I had a great trip to Chicago. I saw the Sears Tower and Wrigley Field.

Inconsistent example

In a representative democracy, voters are entitled to elect their leaders. We should become familiar with the issues and decide which candidate gets our vote.

Edited example

In a representative democracy, we are entitled to elect our leaders. We should become familiar with the issues and decide which candidate gets our vote.

Consistency in point of view is important to make your message clear.

▶ Jargon

Occasionally, your audience allows you to use words that are specific to a profession or hobby. This is called *jargon*. If you are writing a letter to the coach of the football team, for example, you could use language that is specific to football, like "punt," "two-point conversion," and "huddle." If you are writing an essay for a law class, you may use words specific to the law, like "tort," "continuance," and "plea bargain." However, you have to know your audience well if you plan to use jargon, because those readers who do not know the specialized vocabulary will not understand what you have to say. If you must include jargon in your writing, it is always a good idea to include an explanation in the text, unless you are addressing a highly specialized audience.

Example

When the players huddle, or gather together on the field to plan a play, they speak in code.

Exercise 5

Circle the letter of the jargon used in the sentences below. Hint: look at the word choices to see which of them is used only for one specific occupation. Answers can be found at the end of the lesson.

21. The next player to go to bat on the team is a switch-hitter.
   a. player
   b. bat
   c. team
   d. switch-hitter

22. The carpenter used a mortise to fit the two boards together at an angle.
   a. carpenter
   b. mortise
   c. boards
   d. angle

23. The lawyer requested a continuance because she was still interviewing witnesses.
   a. lawyer
   b. continuance
   c. interviewing
   d. witnesses

24. The goalie raised his glove because the opposing forward entered the crease.
   a. goalie
   b. glove
   c. forward
   d. crease

25. The riders stayed together in the peloton, waiting until they approached the finish line to begin sprinting.
   a. riders
   b. peloton
   c. finish line
   d. sprinting

▶ Gender-Neutral Language

You must consider all potential members of your audience when writing; some readers are offended by gender-biased language. Using a masculine pronoun to refer to both sexes and adding diminutive prefixes or suffixes to nouns can alienate your reader. In fact, the term "humankind" is increasingly used to replace "mankind" in academic discourse. Many performing artists, regardless of whether they are male or female, prefer to be called "actors." To appeal to the broadest audience, it is wise to consider how to make your language gender-neutral. If you simply use both masculine and feminine pronouns every time, it can make the sentence awkward.

Example
When a traveler arrives in a foreign country, he or she should spend some time orienting himself or herself with a map and making plans to see sights he or she might find interesting.

Edited example
Travelers in foreign countries should spend some time with a map making plans to see interesting sights.

▶ Word Choice

Every word you write involves a choice on your part. Mark Twain said, "The difference between the right word and the almost right word is the difference between lightning and the lightning bug." With over 650,000 words in the English language to choose from, your choice can be tricky. Good word choices are made with the tone of the piece, the audience, and the purpose in mind.

In a first draft, it can be paralyzing to consider all the aspects of a piece before putting words on paper. Don't worry about voice, language, and word choice at first. Consider your audience and purpose, and then get your thoughts on paper. In the revision process you can shape your words to say exactly what you mean. The revision process is where the craft of writing takes place, where you consider how to make your piece as clear, precise, and graceful as you can.

Good word choices require a large vocabulary. Anything you can do to increase the number of words that you know is a good idea. Keep a list of words that you come across that you don't know and look them up in the dictionary. Practice using specific language instead of lazy language—like slang and colloquialisms—in your everyday communications. Continue to work on saying what you mean clearly and directly; try not to offend your audience by patronizing them or using inaccurate or gender-specific language.

▶ Style

Style is one of the central goals of a good writer. When you create a piece of writing that accomplishes all you set out to accomplish, includes no words that stray from your purpose, is logically coherent and graceful without excess, then you have achieved style. Notice the phrase, "create a piece of writing." Style rarely just happens. Instead, your writing has to be worked at, crafted, rewritten, revised, and rearranged. Your first draft is like the piece of marble that sculptors select. They look it over and visualize how to begin, and then they start carving with large tools like hammers or chisels. As the sculpture progresses, the sculptors use finer and finer tools, removing smaller and smaller pieces of marble, until they reach the final stage, when they polish the sculpture and place it on its base for display. Marble sculptures are beautiful to look at, are completely finished, and serve the purpose of portraying a subject—a person or an object—clearly and beautifully. Your writing should go through a similar process of close revision until the final product is also beautiful to look at, completely revised, and serves its purpose.

Summary

As you write and revise using the techniques in this lesson, you will improve your style, your tone, your voice, and your word choices. It will be evident in your writing that you have made every effort to keep your audience engaged.

▶ Answers

Exercise 1
1. a.
2. b.
3. a.
4. b.
5. b.

Exercise 2
6. b.
7. a.
8. b.
9. b.
10. a.

Exercise 3
11. b.
12. a.
13. b.
14. a.
15. a.

Exercise 4
16. a.
17. b.
18. a.
19. a.
20. b.

Exercise 5
21. d.
22. b.
23. b.
24. d.
25. b.

8 ▶ Turning Passive Verbs into Active Verbs

LESSON SUMMARY

In this lesson, you will learn to revise your writing to change the passive voice to the active voice and capture your reader's interest and attention.

When the subject performs the action expressed in the verb, the verb is in the active voice. When the subject receives the action of the verb, the verb is in the passive voice.

Example of Active Voice

The hunter shot the bird.

> The subject *hunter* performs the action expressed in the verb *shot*.

Example of Passive Voice

The bird was shot by the hunter.

> The subject *bird* receives the action of being *shot*.

In general, using the active voice makes for cleaner and clearer writing. It is clearer because it is more specific, and cleaner because the active voice usually uses fewer words.

Example
The table was set by George. (six words)

Revised Example
George set the table. (four words)

Example
The dinner was cooked by Eileen. (six words)

Revised Example
Eileen cooked the dinner. (four words)

Example
The sugar crop on the coast was damaged by stormy weather. (eleven words)

Revised Example
The stormy weather damaged the sugar crop on the coast. (ten words)

Example
The game was won by the Seattle Mariners. (eight words)

Revised Example
The Seattle Mariners won the game. (six words)

Exercise 1

Select the letter for the sentence that uses the active voice in each of the sentence pairs in this exercise. Answers can be found at the end of the lesson.

1. a. Escobar held the phone.
   b. The phone was held by Escobar.

2. a. The night was filled by the sound of the stray cat's howling.
   b. The sound of the stray cat's howling filled the night.

3. a. The pilot was asked by the control tower to delay the flight.
   b. The control tower asked the pilot to delay the flight.

4. a. The surprise party was organized by Jamie's mother.
   b. Jamie's mother organized the surprise party.

5. a. Many consider Alex to be the best shortstop in the league.
   b. Alex is considered by many to be the best shortstop in the league.

Active voice is clear and concise, two trademarks of good writing. In some situations, however, passive voice is acceptable. For example, when the actor who performed the action is not known, or when the writer does not want to reveal the actor for effect, it is appropriate to use the passive voice.

Example
My backpack was stolen.
   In this sentence, the person who stole the backpack is not known, so the passive voice is acceptable.

Passive voice is correct in some other situations as well. Occasionally, a sentence constructed in the passive voice will be shorter than an active construction.

Example of Active Voice
The creators of the computer game told the players to download their personal statistics before they began to play. (nineteen words)

Example of Passive Voice
The players were told to download their personal statistics before they began to play. (fourteen words)

Example of Active Voice
The framer framed the house, the roofers put the roof on, and the construction crew made it ready to be occupied. (twenty-one words)

Example of Passive Voice
The house was framed, roofed, and made ready to be occupied. (eleven words)

The choice whether to use active or passive voice is a matter of style rather than correctness. However, if the passive voice is used too often, it makes for weak and awkward passages. In the same way that good writing has variety in aspects like sentence length and word choice, it also should have variety in its voice. Long passages in which all the verbs are passive will make your readers look for another way to spend their time.

Example in the passive voice
Sam was brought by his mother, Joan, for his first haircut. His hair was cut by the barber, and then he was given a lollipop by the receptionist. Sam was nervous when he saw the scissors so close to his head, but he was reassured by his older brother that haircuts are no big deal.

Example in the active voice
Sam's mother, Joan, brought him for his first haircut. The barber cut his hair, and then the receptionist gave him a lollipop. Sam was nervous when he saw the scissors so close to his head, but his older brother reassured him that haircuts are no big deal.

▶ Revising the Passive Voice

To turn a passive sentence into an active sentence, the subject of the verb must perform the action. Move the object of the passive sentence so that it appears before the verb and becomes the subject. Eliminate the form of the verb *to be*, and turn the subject of the passive sentence into the object.

Imagine that the verb is the middle of a seesaw. The subject of a passive sentence is on the left and the object is on the right. To turn the sentence into an active sentence, they must switch places.

Example of passive construction
The mail was opened by my daughter.
  Subject   verb   object

Switch the places of the subject and object to eliminate the form of "to be."

Example of active construction
My daughter opened the mail.
  Subject   verb object

Example of passive construction
Bernie was taught to read by his first grade teacher.
Subject verb   object

Example of active construction
His first grade teacher taught Bernie to read.
      Subject verb   object

Exercise 2

Revise the following sentences to change the passive voice to the active voice. Write the revised sentence on the lines provided. Answers can be found at the end of the lesson.

6. A firefly was captured by the boy.

_____

7. The lasagna was prepared by Dan.

_____

8. A memo was delivered to me by the director of marketing.

_____

_____

9. He was ordered to move by his superior.

_____

10. Several novels were read by the book club.

_____

▶ Revising State-of-Being Verbs

State-of-being verbs are forms of the verb "to be." The table at the bottom of this page lists all of the state of being verbs.

Unnecessary state-of-being verbs slow the action of a sentence. To keep your reader involved and to keep your sentences as concise as possible, revise state-of-being verbs whenever possible. The following paragraph demonstrates the overuse of state-of-being verbs.

Example
The fall foliage in New England was beautiful. The trees were orange and yellow. At the top of a hill was one particularly interesting tree. Its leaves were shaped like hearts and were deep red. The sun was bright and the air was cold, but it was a good day to hike.

Revised Example
The fall foliage in New England looked beautiful. Orange and yellow leaves filled the trees. One particularly stately tree—with deep red, heart-shaped leaves—stood at the top of a hill. An ineffective, but bright, sun made it a perfect day for hiking.

SUBJECT	PRESENT	PAST	PAST PARTICIPLE	FUTURE	CONDITIONAL
I	am	was	have been	will be	would be
You	are	were	have been	will be	would be
He/She/It	is	was	has been	will be	would be
We	are	were	have been	will be	would be
You (plural)	are	were	have been	will be	would be
They	are	were	have been	will be	would be

The second paragraph moves along more quickly and conveys the feeling in a livelier manner. It is also more concise, trimming the first paragraph from fifty-three words to forty-three.

▶ Turning Verbs into Nouns

Occasionally, it may be tempting to turn verbs into nouns as a way of sounding more "academic" or "intellectual," but it usually makes the writing less clear. Using "sophisticated" vocabulary does not improve upon good, clear writing.

Example with verbs as nouns
The front office made the decision to begin a feasibility study regarding the development of a better mousetrap.

Revised example
The front office decided to study the feasibility of developing a better mousetrap.

▶ Adding Unnecessary Auxiliary Verbs

Auxiliary verbs such as *have, had, is, are, was, were, will, would* and so on are unnecessary if they don't help convey the meaning of the sentence. Eliminate them if the meaning of the sentence stays the same.

Example
Every day we would eat donuts before practice.

Revised example
Every day we ate donuts before practice.

Example
George had gone to get coffee, but he had forgotten his money.

Revised example
George went to get coffee but forgot his money.

Exercise 3
Revise the following sentences to eliminate unnecessary state-of-being and auxiliary verbs. Write the new sentence on the line provided. Suggested answers can be found at the end of the lesson.

11. The test was on the Civil War.

_____

12. I had hoped to find my necklace by the swimming pool.

_____

_____

13. We would run twice around the track during our lunch break.

_____

_____

14. If you want to be eating ice cream, let's go get some.

_____

_____

15. I had had the flu, but now I am being healthy with what I eat.

_____

_____

▶ Starting with *there* or *it*

Sentences sometimes unnecessarily begin with phrases like *there is, there was, there were, it is,* and *it was.* The use of these phrases delays the beginning of the idea in a sentence. Eliminating them during revision will make your writing clearer and more direct.

Example
There are a number of people who can touch their noses with their tongues.

Revised example
A number of people can touch their noses with their tongues.

Example
It was too rainy of a day for soccer.

Revised example
The day was too rainy for soccer.

Example
There were eight or nine children home with the flu.

Revised example
Eight or nine children were home with the flu.

▶ Use Lively Verbs

Clear writing means the reader understands what you mean. Many verbs do not clearly express the idea of the sentence as well as a livelier verb could.

Example
One cook does the prep work, one is the line cook who uses the barbecue, and one does the desserts.

Revised example
One cook prepares the food to be cooked, one grills the food to perfection, and one cuts desserts and arranges them on the plate.

Use lively verbs to be specific and entertaining. Why should someone *walk* when they can *stroll, meander, stride, clamber, skip, hike, saunter, amble, march, totter, toddle,* or *stagger?*

Exercise 4
Revise the following sentences to turn nouns into verbs and to eliminate *there* or *it* at the beginning of the sentences. Write the revised sentence on the lines provided. Suggested answers can be found at the end of the lesson.

16. There are twenty different drills on sale at the hardware store.

_____

_____

17. We did a study on frogs in the rain forest.

_____

18. It was too cold of a day to go hiking.

_____

19. The development of the child was faster than the other second grade students.

_____

_____

20. There can be no other way to climb the mountain.

_____

_____

Summary

This lesson has shown you how to change passive verbs and state-of-being verbs into active verbs. While there are situations when the passive voice is the best way to express yourself, but in general, the active voice does a better job of keeping your reader reading. Editing unnecessary auxiliary verbs to make your writing direct and concise has been covered as well.

▶ Answers

Exercise 1
1. a.
2. b.
3. b.
4. b.
5. a.

Exercise 2
6. The boy captured a firefly.
7. Dan prepared the lasagna.
8. The director of marketing delivered a memo to me.
9. His superior ordered him to move.
10. The book club read several novels.

Exercise 3
11. The test covered the Civil War.
12. I hoped to find my necklace by the swimming pool.
13. We sprinted twice around the track during our lunch break.
14. If you want to eat ice cream, let's go get some.
15. I had the flu, but now I am eating healthily.

Exercise 4
16. Twenty different drills are on sale at the hardware store.
17. We studied frogs in the rain forest.
18. The day was too cold to go hiking.
19. The child developed faster than the other second grade students.
20. No other way to climb the mountain exists.

9 ▶ Making Sure Subjects and Verbs Agree

LESSON SUMMARY

In this lesson, you will learn to proofread and revise your writing so that the subject and verb of each sentence are in agreement.

The subject of a sentence is the person or thing doing the action, and the verb is the action, as discussed in Lesson 2. The subject and the verb have matching forms to show a relationship between them. If the subject is singular, the verb has to be singular. If the subject is plural, the verb has to be plural. This is called agreement in number.

Example

Singular
One dog sleeps.

Plural
Two dogs sleep.

The subject and verb would not be in agreement if the sentence were, "One dog sleep," or "Two dogs sleeps."

Singular verbs often end in "-s," such as: he *lifts*, she *carries*, it *hurts*. Plural verbs usually do not end in "-s," such as: they *lift*, they *carry*, they *hurt*. The exceptions are verbs used with "I" and the singular "you," such as: I *lift*, you *lift*, I *carry*, you *carry*, I *hurt*, you *hurt*.

Exercise 1

Select the correct verb for each of the following sentences. Answers can be found at the end of the lesson.

1. Claire is such a good cook that she rarely (**a.** follow **b.** follows) recipes.

2. They eat so much turkey that it (**a.** feel **b.** feels) as if they are going to burst.

3. On the bus, Phuong always (**a.** sit **b.** sits) toward the back.

4. The locksmith took out her keys and said, "This lock (**a.** opens **b.** open) easily."

5. I (**a.** has **b.** have) never been to the top of the Empire State Building.

6. Toby and Kurt (**a.** leaves **b.** leave) for Central America today.

7. We (**a.** applies **b.** apply) for the new grant money today.

8. Sheila (**a.** paints **b.** paint) my nails every other Saturday.

9. Tyler and Casey (**a.** shares **b.** share) the NYPD baseball hat.

10. The oak trees always (**a.** looks **b.** look) beautiful in the twilight.

▶ Past Tense

Almost all past tense verbs have the same form in the singular and plural.

SINGULAR	PLURAL
I looked	They looked
Diane spoke	Dean and Jeff spoke
The cat was	The cats were*
It was	They were*

*One exception is the verb *to be* which changes form in the present tense and past tense in both the first and third person.

PRESENT TENSE OF *TO BE*		PAST TENSE OF *TO BE*	
first person:			
I am	we are	I was	we were
second person:			
you are	you are	you were	you were
third person:			
he, she, it is	they are	he, she, it was	they were

Common errors with *to be* include *you was*, *we was*, and *they was*. While there are some clear-cut examples of agreement in number, there are often exceptions to the rule that can present difficulties in agreement. The sections that follow give you some of the common problems that writers often have with agreement.

▶ Contractions

Not all contractions present a problem, but two pairs of them consistently cause problems.

SINGULAR	PLURAL
Doesn't	Don't
Wasn't	Weren't

Example

She *doesn't* want to drive by herself, but they *don't* want to go at all.

Example

Bill *wasn't* on the roller coaster when it stopped. Campbell and Ken *weren't* even in line yet.

Exercise 2

Select the correct form of the verb in each of the following sentences. Answers can be found at the end of the lesson.

11. (**a.** Doesn't **b.** Don't) the owner of the car with the flat tire live near here?

12. (**a.** Who's **b.** Who are) the students in the decorating committee?

13. The photograph (**a.** doesn't **b.** don't) look anything like her.

14. The beach (**a.** wasn't **b.** weren't) crowded today.

15. Phil and Leda (**a.** wasn't **b.** weren't) late for the movie.

When revising your writing, read the whole phrase instead of the contractions. This will help you to locate errors in agreement. Contractions are considered informal, anyway, so if you can avoid using them, you will eliminate a source of error in both punctuation and agreement.

▶ Phrases Following the Subject

Sometimes the subject and verb in a sentence are split up by a phrase. The subject does not change in number when a phrase follows it.

Example

Dennis, in his overalls, looks like a farmer.

Phrases can be misleading, especially if they contain a plural word, such as "overalls." The verb always agrees with its subject, not with modifiers. Remove the phrase *in his overalls* and the agreement between subject and verb is much easier to see and hear:

Dennis looks like a farmer.

Example

Mayra and Gabriel, posing in their costumes for the play, really look like Romeo and Juliet.

Phrases that separate the subject and verb are not always set off by commas.

Example

We know that one of the police officers at the scene was injured.

The subject of the sentence is *one*, so the verb must be the singular *was*.

Exercise 3

Select the correct verb for each of the following sentences. Answers can be found at the end of the lesson.

16. If you (**a.** was **b.** were) in class, why didn't you say "present?"

17. We could hardly believe that the color of his stereo speakers (**a.** was **b.** were) silver.

18. The decision of the referee, after checking the rule book, (**a.** stands **b.** stand).

19. The state income tax, combined with real estate taxes and lottery monies, (**a.** pays **b.** pay) most of the cost of our public schools.

20. We, the members of the Step Dancing Team, including outgoing president Jennifer Perez, (**a.** wishes **b.** wish) you continued success.

To check for agreement when revising, isolate the subject and verb and read them together without all the phrases.

▶ Special Singular Subjects

Some nouns are singular even though they end in *s*. We think of them as a single thing even though they take the plural form.

measles	news	sports
mumps	physics	athletics
civics	politics	acoustics
mathematics	statistics	gymnastics
tactics		

Example
Politics is a dirty business.

Example
Physics is one of the more difficult classes.

Most of the nouns on the list above are singular only, although some can be singular or plural depending on their use in the sentence.

Example of singular use
Gymnastics is an excellent way to stay limber.

Example of plural use
Rhythmic and toddler gymnastics are the most popular programs at the gym.

Some nouns that do not end in *s* but name a group of people or things also can take a singular verb, like *jury, band, family, committee, club, team, herd,* and *crowd*. These are called *collective nouns*. They are considered singular when the group acts together as a single unit.

Example
The jury *is* ready to hear testimony.

Example
The club typically *travels* by bus.

An amount of money or time also takes a singular verb as long as the amount is a single measure.

Examples
Seven dollars *is* the cost of admission.

Three hours *was* the time of the race from start to finish.

Three-fifths of my work shift *is* spent cleaning up.

When revising your writing, examine the subject of each sentence to determine if it requires a singular verb. Usually, the strategy of reading your draft aloud will help you hear if a subject and verb do not agree.

Exercise 4
Select the correct verb for each sentence. Answers can be found at the end of the lesson.

21. The team (**a.** make **b.** makes) money by selling magazine subscriptions.

22. Half of the television programs (**a.** show **b.** shows) acts of violence.

23. The knives (**a.** is **b.** are) in the drawer.

24. The committee (**a.** votes **b.** vote) to change the by-laws.

25. The scalper said, "Thirty seven dollars (**a.** buys **b.** buy) you a front row seat."

▶ Singular and Plural Pronouns

Pronouns, like regular nouns, can be singular or plural and must agree with the verb. Pronouns that do not refer to specific people or things, also known as *indefinite pronouns*, present the greatest difficulty for subject/verb agreement.

SINGULAR INDEFINITE PRONOUNS

each	anyone	either
one	anybody	neither
no one	someone	everyone
nobody	somebody	everybody

Example
No one in the movie *screams* louder than Theresa.

Pronouns and their verbs can also be separated by phrases. It can be even more confusing if the phrase contains a plural noun.

Example
Either of the coffee makers *brews* good coffee.

PLURAL INDEFINITE PRONOUNS

both	many
few	several

Example
Both of the wrestlers *want* to win the match.

Some pronouns can take either the singular or plural form depending on how they are used.

SINGULAR/PLURAL PRONOUNS

all	none
any	some
most	

These pronouns are considered singular when they refer to a quantity and plural when they refer to a number of individual items.

Example of quantity
All of the cake was eaten.
   All refers to the quantity of the whole cake that was eaten, so the singular verb *was* is used.

Example of number
All of the magazines were scattered across the floor.
   All refers to the number of individual magazines, so the plural verb *were* is used.

Exercise 5
Select the correct verb form for each of the following sentences. Answers can be found at the end of the lesson.

26. Some of the paint (**a.** is **b.** are) dry.

27. One of the new employees (**a.** plays **b.** play) guitar.

28. Someone from the two classes (**a.** needs **b.** need) to volunteer.

29. Several of the motorcycles (**a.** are **b.** is) in need of repairs.

30. All of our profits (**a.** goes **b.** go) to charity.

► Compound Subjects

When more than one noun or pronoun is doing the action represented by one verb in a sentence, those nouns or pronouns are called compound subjects. If the two nouns or pronouns are joined by *and*, they agree with a plural verb.

Examples
Josh and Susan eat tamales.

He and she spend Saturdays with friends.

If two singular nouns are joined by *or* or *nor*, they require a singular verb.

Examples
Josh or Susan eats tamales.

Neither he nor she spends Saturdays with friends.

When revising, it helps to think of compound subjects joined by *or* or *nor* as separate sentences.

Example
Josh eats tamales. Susan eats tamales.

Singular and plural subjects joined by *or* or *nor* require a verb that agrees with the subject closest to the verb.

Examples
Neither the players nor the coach likes to play in the rain.

Neither the coach nor the players like to play in the rain.

► Questions

Usually in a sentence, the subject comes before the verb. With questions, however, the verb usually comes first. This can make agreement between the subject and verb hard to figure out.

Example
What are the differences between Greek and Italian food?
The subject of that sentence is *differences*, which is plural; therefore the verb must be plural.

Example
When does Henry get back from his trip?
The subject of that sentence is *Henry*, which is singular, so the verb *does* must be singular.

If you find it too confusing to decide which form of the verb is correct in your draft, try turning the question into a statement on a separate piece of paper. Statements are often an easier form to check for agreement.

EXAMPLE IN QUESTION FORM	EXAMPLE IN STATEMENT FORM
(Is, Are) some of the players injured?	Some of the players are injured.
(Does, Do) each of the bedrooms have a T.V?	Each of the bedrooms does have a T.V.
(Has, Have) several books been lost?	Several books have been lost.

▶ Inverted Sentences

Inverted sentences contain subjects that follow the verb, just like questions. As usual, locate the subject of the sentence and make sure the verb agrees.

Example
Here are the keys to the car.
    The subject is *keys*, which is plural, so the plural *are* is used.

Here is the key to the car.
    The subject *key* is singular, so the singular *is* is used.

Examples
There goes the train.

There go the trains.

Examples
Suddenly, out of the woods comes the grizzly bear.

Suddenly, out of the woods come the grizzly bears.

Examples
Along with the questionnaire goes our brochure.

Along with the questionnaire go two brochures.

Exercise 6

Select the correct verb for each of the following sentences. Answers can be found at the end of the lesson.

31. Beside the couch (**a.** stands **b.** stand) an end table.

32. When (**a.** does **b.** do) we have a lunch break?

33. Neither the doctor nor the patients (**a.** prefers **b.** prefer) the new lounge area.

34. Jamie and Deeptha (**a.** wants **b.** want) to go skiing.

35. Here (**a.** is **b.** are) the hot dogs you ordered.

Summary

This lesson has taught you about singular and plural nouns, verbs, and pronouns and how to make them agree. You learned how to make past tense verbs agree and what to do with some special singular subjects. Also, you learned what to do with sentences that have unusual structures, such as questions or inverted sentences.

▶ Answers

Exercise 1

1. b.
2. b.
3. b.
4. a.
5. b.
6. b.
7. b.
8. a.
9. b.
10. b.

Exercise 2

11. a.
12. b.
13. a.
14. a.
15. b.

Exercise 3

16. b.
17. a.
18. a.
19. a.
20. b.

Exercise 4

21. b.
22. a.
23. b.
24. a.
25. a.

Exercise 5

26. a.
27. a.
28. a.
29. a.
30. b.

Exercise 6

31. a.
32. b.
33. b.
34. b.
35. b.

10▶ Making Sure Nouns and Pronouns Agree

LESSON SUMMARY

This lesson will show you how to proofread, revise, and edit your work to be sure that your nouns and pronouns agree.

A pronoun is a word that replaces one or more nouns. Pronouns must agree with nouns in a sentence in much the same way that subjects must agree with verbs.

Example

The students complained to the principal about the quality of the cafeteria food. They claim that he isn't concerned about whether it is healthy for them to eat.

The pronouns *they* and *them* replace the noun *students*. The pronoun *he* replaces the noun *principal*. The pronoun *it* replaces the noun *food*.

Example

The clown wore big shoes and a big nose. They were both red.

The pronoun *they* replaces the nouns *shoes* and *nose*.

A pronoun can also replace another pronoun.

Example
One of the DVD players is disconnected. It is missing a cable.

The pronoun *it* replaces the pronoun *one* in this sentence.

▶ Antecedents

An *antecedent* is the word to which the pronoun refers. In the previous example, *one* is the antecedent of *it*. To use pronouns correctly, you must make sure they agree in number with their antecedent. In other words, a singular antecedent requires a singular pronoun and a plural antecedent requires a plural pronoun. When a noun is the antecedent, it is usually pretty clear whether it is singular or plural. It gets more confusing when a pronoun is the antecedent. Thankfully, the rules for noun/pronoun agreement are very similar to the rules for subject/verb agreement.

▶ Singular Pronouns

Here is a list of singular pronouns:

each	anybody	everyone
one	either	anyone
no one	somebody	neither
everybody	nobody	someone

A pronoun with one of the words from this list as its antecedent must be singular.

Example
Each of the women tried to swim *her* fastest and win the race.

Example
Nobody brought *his* or *her* favorite dessert to the potluck dinner.

▶ Plural Pronouns

Here is a list of plural pronouns:

several	few	both	many

If two or more singular nouns or pronouns are joined by *and,* use a plural pronoun.

Example
If *he* and *she* were on time, *they* wouldn't have missed the bus.

Example
Brad and *Janet* believe in *their* chances to win the election.

If two or more singular nouns or pronouns are joined by *or,* use a singular pronoun.

Example
Walt or *Jim* will provide *his* expertise.

Two or more singular pronoun antecedents followed by singular pronouns can make for some awkward sentences. It follows the pronoun agreement rule, but you should consider revising any sentences that use this construction.

Example
He or *she* wants *his* or *her* notebook back.

If a singular and a plural noun or pronoun are joined by *or* or *nor,* the pronoun agrees with its closest antecedent.

Example

Neither the photographer nor his models like the setting for the shoot.

Example

Neither the models nor the photographer likes the setting for the shoot.

Example

David disagrees with the council about how to proceed. Either *he* or *they* will get *their* way.

Example

The council disagrees with David about how to proceed. Either *they* or *he* will get *his* way.

While it is important to know the rules when using pronouns, occasionally their use does not make for clear and concise writing. When editing and revising your paper, rearranging the structure of a sentence or paragraph can allow you to eliminate awkward pronouns.

Exercise 1

Select the correct pronoun in each of the following sentences. Answers can be found at the end of the lesson.

1. Anyone who wants a ride to the concert must put (**his, their**) name on the sign-up sheet.

2. Neither Alex nor his classmates could find (**his, their**) homework.

3. Almost anybody can make (**his, their**) own birdhouse.

4. Melissa or Tamica will loan you (**her, their**) pencil.

5. Frank and Andre made (**his, their**) script into a video.

▶ Cases of Pronouns

Personal pronouns come in three cases: *nominative, objective,* and *possessive.* The table below shows the cases of all the personal pronouns, both singular and plural.

NOMINATIVE		OBJECTIVE	POSSESSIVE
First person:	I	me	my
Second person:	We	us	our
	You	you	your
Third person:	He	him	his
	She	her	hers
	They	them	their
	It	it	its

Nominative Case Pronouns

The subject of a verb is in the nominative case. When a pronoun is the subject of the verb in a sentence, the pronoun must be in the nominative case. Most writers do this without thinking.

Example
He is a good worker.

Not "*him* is a good worker," or "*his* is a good worker." *He* is the subject, so it appears in the nominative case.

When the pronoun follows a linking verb, however, the correct usage may sound awkward.

Examples
The landscape architect who designed the garden is *he*.

"It is *I*," said my brother.

Objective Case Pronouns

Objective case pronouns are used as the object in a sentence. They usually follow an action verb or act as the object of a preposition.

Example
The crossing guard gave *him* a wave.

The pronoun *him* follows the action word *gave*, so it is in the objective case.

Example
We went to the park with Jordan and *her*.

The pronoun *her* is the object of the preposition *with*, so it is in the objective case.

Example
This is between you and *me*.

The pronoun *me* is the object of the preposition *between*, so it is in the objective case.

Possessive Case Pronouns

Possessive case pronouns show possession.

Example
The shoes are *his*.

The shoes belong to him, so he possesses them. The possessive pronoun *his* is used.

Example
That is *our* way of celebrating the new season.

Whose way is it? The way belongs to us, so it is *our* way.

The possessive case rarely presents problems. The nominative and objective cases, however, can be tricky.

▶ Pronoun Case Problems

Most writers do not have agreement problems when pronouns are used alone in a sentence.

Example
He sat at the table.

When pronouns are used with a noun or another pronoun, it can be confusing.

Examples of incorrect usage
The taxi driver drove my neighbor and I to the store.

Jimmy and me are going to work in Georgia.

The mechanic spoke to he and I about the repairs.

One strategy for ensuring that you are using the correct case with your pronouns is to separate the sentence into two sentences.

Examples of separated sentences
The taxi driver drove my neighbor to the store.

The taxi driver drove I to the store.

   The second sentence should read: The taxi driver drove *me* to the store.

Jimmy is going to work in Georgia.

Me is going to work in Georgia.

   The second sentence should read: *I am* going to work in Georgia.

The mechanic spoke to he about the repairs.
   This sentence should read: the mechanic spoke to *him* about the repairs.

The mechanic spoke to I about the repairs.
   This sentence should read: the mechanic spoke to *me* about the repairs.

   When a sentence contains the preposition *between*, splitting sentences does not work. Try substituting *with* for *between*.

Example of incorrect usage
The problem is between she and I.

Examples of separated sentences
The problem is with she.
   This sentence should read: The problem is with *her*.

The problem is with I.
   This sentence should read: The problem is with *me*.

Example of correct sentence
The problem is between her and me.

Exercise 2

Select the correct pronouns in each of the following sentences. Answers can be found at the end of the lesson.

6. The conductor let (**he, him**) and (**I, me**) stand at the podium.

7. My good friend and (**I, me**) want to join the chess club.

8. "It is (**I, me**)," he said. "I have come to vote."

9. Deena and (**she, her**) went to the playground with Frances and (**I, me**).

10. Have you heard the gossip about (**she, her**) and (**they, them**)?

11. Neither my teacher nor my classmates know what (**he, they**) will read next.

12. The guests thanked Gita and (**she, her**) for the party.

13. What were you telling Earl and (**we, us**) before?

14. I remember Jan and (**she, her**).

15. You and (**he, him**) have been studying all weekend.

▶ Ambiguous Pronoun Reference

Sometimes a sentence is written with more than one antecedent, making it ambiguous. Ambiguous means it can have two or more possible meanings;

therefore, the antecedent to which the pronoun refers is unclear.

Example
Markella screamed at Stephanie, and *she* seemed scared.

It is unclear whether the pronoun *she* refers to Stephanie or Markella.

Example
Edgar told Greg *he* was supposed to leave.

It is unclear whether the pronoun *he* refers to Edgar or Greg.

Example
Separate the fern from the flower and replant *it*.

It is unclear whether *it* refers to the fern or the flower.

To eliminate this problem, revise your sentences so that it is clear to which antecedent the pronoun refers.

Examples of revised sentences
Markella screamed at Stephanie, and Stephanie seemed scared.

Edgar was supposed to leave, so he told Greg.

Replant the flower after separating it from the fern.

▶ Improper Reflexive Pronouns

A reflexive pronoun is one that includes the word *self* or *selves*. The table below shows the most common reflexive pronouns.

myself	yourself	himself
herself	ourselves	themselves

Nominative case pronouns are never used to make reflexive pronouns.

Example
I took the ball Iself.

In fact, to create reflexive pronouns, you add *self* or *selves* to the objective case pronouns for the third person, which are *him, her,* and *them.* You add *self* or *selves* to the first and second person in the possessive case, which are *my, our,* and *your.* If this sounds confusing, look at the table of pronouns in the three cases in this lesson, and use your ear. You cannot make the pronouns *me, us, you, his,* or *their* reflexive.

Examples of incorrect usage
They were determined to complete the project *theirselves.*

I will drink the last of the milk *meself.*

Boris took over the responsibilities *hisself.*

Examples of correct usage
They were determined to complete the project *themselves.*

I will drink the last of the milk *myself.*

Boris took over the responsibilities *himself.*

When a personal pronoun works in a sentence, do not use a reflexive pronoun.

Examples of incorrect usage
The plans to tear down the barn were known only by *ourselves.*

Three good singers and *myself* were chosen for the vocal group.

Examples of correct usage
The plans to tear down the barn were known only by *us*.

Three good singers and *I* were chosen for the vocal group.

Reflexive pronouns should be used only to refer to another word in the same sentence or to emphasize another word. Any other use should be edited and revised from your writing.

Summary

This lesson has shown you how to make your nouns and pronouns agree. You learned about antecedents and the different cases and how to use them correctly in your writing. When you proofread your own writing, try to approach the piece as if you are reading it for the first time. Look for ambiguous or unclear pronoun references and sentences in which nouns and pronouns do not agree. Revise them, and your writing will be clearer and easier to understand.

▶ Answers

Exercise 1
1. his
2. their
3. his
4. her
5. their

Exercise 2
6. him, me
7. I
8. I
9. she, me
10. her, them
11. they
12. her
13. us
14. her
15. he

11 ▶ Using Modifiers

LESSON SUMMARY

In this lesson, you will learn how to insert single-word modifiers—such as adjectives, adverbs, and phrase modifiers—to give your writing accuracy and detail.

Words and phrases that describe other words are called *modifiers*. Adjectives and adverbs are known as single-word modifiers. When revising your writing, correct usage of modifiers should be a top priority.

▶ Adjectives

Adjectives modify a noun or a pronoun in a sentence. They answer one of three questions about another word in the sentence: *which one? what kind?* or *how many?*

Example
I remember the *first* time I drove a car.
   Which time was it? The *first* time.

Example

It was a *green* car.

    What kind of car was it? A *green* car.

Example

I accidentally bumped *three* cars when I parallel parked.

    How many cars did I bump? *Three* cars.

► Adverbs

Adverbs modify verbs, adjectives, and other adverbs.

Example

The man ate *quickly*.

    The adverb *quickly* modifies the verb *ate*.

Example

He made an *extremely* annoying sound.

    The adverb *extremely* modifies the adjective *annoying*.

Example

The other patrons were *quite understandably* disturbed.

    The adverb *quite* modifies the adverb *understandably*.

    Adverbs answer one of four questions about another word in the sentence: *where?*, *when?*, *how?*, and *to what extent?*

Example

I put my carry-on bag *below* the seat.

    Where did I put my carry-on bag? *Below* the seat.

Example

I will need my book *later*.

    When will I need my book? *Later*.

Example

The plane taxied *slowly* to the runway.

    How did the plane taxi to the runway? *Slowly*.

Example

I could *hardly* wait until takeoff.

    To what extent could I wait? *Hardly*.

► Adjective or Adverb?

It can be confusing to determine whether an adjective or an adverb is appropriate in a sentence. Whenever a modifier is placed directly before an action verb, an adjective, or another adverb, it is always an adverb. When an adverb comes after the word it modifies, it can be tempting to use an adjective instead. A common error occurs when writers use an adjective in place of an adverb.

Incorrect Example

Move the piano very *careful*.

    Careful is used incorrectly as an adjective in the sentence.

Edited Example

Move the piano very carefully.

Incorrect Example

We sang as *loud* as we could.

    Loud is used incorrectly as an adjective in the sentence.

Edited Example

We sang as loudly as we could.

► Linking Verbs

An adjective rather than an adverb almost always follows a linking verb. The linking verb *to be* does not cause much confusion, but most of the other linking verbs can also be used as action verbs. Following is a list of confusing linking verbs:

look	appear	smell
stay	grow	seem
sound	feel	taste
remain	become	act

Example
The police officer *appeared* angry.
   Angry is an adjective describing the officer.

Example
The police officer *appeared* suddenly.
   Suddenly is an adverb that tells *how* the officer appeared.

   If you are not sure whether to use an adjective or an adverb following a verb, determine whether the verb is used as a linking verb. If so, use an adjective.

Exercise 1

Select the correct word for each sentence and write whether it is an adjective or an adverb on the line provided. Answers can be found at the end of the lesson.

1. Yelena completed the translation (**easy, easily**).

_____

2. Billy seemed (**nervous, nervously**) as he got up to speak.

_____

3. The manager (**quick, quickly**) made her way to the front desk.

_____

4. Wally's fingerpainting was displayed (**prominent, prominently**) on the fridge.

_____

5. The two boys talked (**loud, loudly**) about the game.

_____

6. Oswald's injury looks (**bad, badly**).

_____

7. The bulldog looked (**shy, shyly**) at his master.

_____

8. Why does every book in this series end so (**sad, sadly**)?

_____

▶ Confusing Adjectives and Adverbs

Fewer and Less

Fewer and *less* are both adjectives, and their use can be confusing. *Fewer* is used to describe things that can be counted. *Less* refers to quantity or degree.

Example
Joan has *fewer* earaches than she used to have.
   You can count the number of earaches, so *fewer* is used.

Example
There has been *less* wind this week.

    Wind cannot be counted. It refers to quantity, as in "how much wind?" *Less* is used.

Example
This project is *less* important than the last.

    Importance cannot be counted. It is a matter of degree, so *less* is used.

This, That, These, and Those

This, *that*, *these*, and *those* are being used as pronouns when they are not modifying another noun in the sentence. When used as adjectives, *this* and *that* modify singular nouns, and *these* and *those* modify plural nouns.

Example
This newspaper is my favorite.

Example
Those dogs keep barking.

    Kind, sort, and *type* require singular modifiers.

Example
This kind tastes like orange.

Example
That sort of bad acting can be hard to watch.

Them

Them is always a pronoun and never an adjective.

Incorrect Example
Are you going with *them* guys?

Edited Example
Are you going with *those* guys?

Edited Example
Are you going with them?

Good, Bad, Well, and Badly

Good and *bad* are adjectives. *Well* and *badly* are adverbs. Occasionally, *good* and *bad* are mistakenly used to describe a verb when *well* or *badly* should be used.

Incorrect Example
The jazz band performed *good* at the conference.

Edited Example
The jazz band performed *well* at the conference.

    Well modifies the verb *performed*.

Example
The tree house was *badly* built.

    Badly modifies the verb *built*.

Example
Lena felt *good* after her massage.

    Good describes how *Lena* feels.

Example
He is a *bad* photographer.

    Bad describes the noun *photographer*.

Real and Really

Real should not be used as an adverb. *Really* is the proper adverbial form.

Incorrect Example
I had a *real* bad accident.

Edited Example
I had a *really* bad accident.

Slow and Slowly

Slow is an adjective and *slowly* is an adverb. A common mistake, and a very public one, has been made on highway signs that instruct drivers to *go slow* or *drive slow*. When you use *slow* in your writing, use it as an adjective. Do not let this common mistake affect your writing. Next time you pass one of those signs, you can take the role of editor and smile to yourself. Just remember to drive *slowly*.

Exercise 2

Select the correct word for each sentence and write whether it is an adjective or an adverb on the line provided. Answers can be found at the end of the lesson.

9. The windshield wipers did not work (**good, well**).

_____

10. There were (**fewer, less**) cars on the road this summer.

_____

11. The damage from the flooding looks (**bad, badly**).

_____

12. Take off (**them, those**) wet shoes.

_____

13. When there is ice on the road, remember to go (**slow, slowly**).

_____

14. The kiwi fruit did not taste (**good, well**).

_____

15. They forgot his birthday, so he feels (**bad, badly**).

_____

16. There were (**fewer, less**) cool breezes on the beach today.

_____

17. It was a (**real, really**) hot day.

_____

18. (**Them, those**) houses are all the same.

_____

▶ Comparative and Superlative

Adjectives and adverbs change form when they are used to compare degrees of qualities. There are three degrees of comparison: *positive, comparative,* and *superlative*. The *comparative* form is used when describing two items. There are two ways to create the comparative form:

- Add *-er* to the modifier if it is a short word of one or two syllables.
- Use the word *more* or the word *less* before the modifier if it is a longer word with more than two syllables.

If you are comparing more than two items, use the *superlative* form. Like the comparative form, the *superlative* form is created in two ways:

- Add *-est* to the modifier if it is a short word of one or two syllables.
- Use the word *most* or *least* before the modifier if it is a longer word with more than two syllables.

Examples are provided in the table below.

MODIFIER	COMPARATIVE	SUPERLATIVE
shiny	shinier	shiniest
funny	funnier	funniest
strong	stronger	strongest
intelligent	more (or less) intelligent	most (or least) intelligent
accurately	more (or less) accurately	most (or least) accurately
incredible	more (or less) incredible	most (or least) incredible

If these rules held true all the time, then the *comparative* form and the *superlative* form would be easy to master. However, there are exceptions to these rules. Some modifiers change form completely. Examples are provided in the table below.

MODIFIER	COMPARATIVE	SUPERLATIVE
good	better	best
well	better	best
many	more	most
much	more	most
bad	worse	worst
little	less or lesser	least
far	farther or further	farthest or furthest

Examples
Air freight is a *better* way to ship than on the ground. (comparing two ways)

Blue looks *better* than any other color we've seen. (comparing two colors many times)

Grilling salmon is the *best* way to cook it. (comparing more than one way)

Stevenson High School is the *best* high school in the Bronx. (comparing more than two high schools)

▶ Avoiding Double Comparisons

A double comparison occurs when a writer uses *more* with a modifier containing the comparative ending *-er* or *most* with a modifier containing the superlative ending *-est*.

Incorrect Example
Julio is *more sleepier* than I am.

   Sleepier already implies *more*, so it is unnecessary.

Edited Example
Julio is *sleepier* than I am.

Incorrect Example
That song was the *least likeliest* Grammy winner I have ever heard.

Edited Example
That song was the *least likely* Grammy winner I have ever heard.

▶ Avoiding Double Negatives

When a negative word is added to a statement that is already negative, a *double negative* results. Double negatives are not always obvious, like the use of *not no*.

Incorrect Example
There is *not no* room in the car.

Incorrect Example
The school *doesn't* have *no* textbooks for Latin.

   Remember, the contraction *doesn't* is short for *does not*.

   Often, double negatives occur when words that function as negative words, like *hardly* or *barely*, are used with other negative words.

Incorrect Example
I *can't hardly* hear you in this heavy rain.

Edited Example
I *can hardly* hear you in this heavy rain.

Incorrect Example
The snow *won't barely* cover the walkway.

Edited Example
The snow *will barely* cover the walkway.

▶ Avoiding Illogical Comparisons

Other or Else
Use the words *other* or *else* when making comparisons between an individual member and the rest of a group.

Incorrect Example
Matthew is smarter than any man.

   In the above example, Matthew himself is a man, so the comparison implies that Matthew is smarter than himself.

Edited Example
Matthew is smarter than any *other* man.

Incorrect Example
Lily is as talented as anyone in her violin class.

Edited Example
Lily is as talented as anyone *else* in her violin class.

Clearly Stated Comparisons
To avoid confusing your reader, clearly state both parts of a comparison.

Example
I like her more than Mrs. Schnitzer.

Edited Examples

I like her more than Mrs. Schnitzer does.

I like her more than I like Mrs. Schnitzer.

▶ Misplaced Single-Word Modifiers

The clearest way to use modifiers is to place them as closely as possible to the words they describe. A misplaced modifier can confuse your reader..

Example

Evelyn *only* ate the fried rice.

This sentence is confusing because the modifier is placed close to the verb *ate*. If the intended meaning of the sentence is that Evelyn did not eat any other dish, place the modifier closer to *fried rice*.

Edited Example

Evelyn ate *only* the fried rice.

Example

Peyton *almost* passed three classes.

The sentence above implies that Peyton did not pass any of the three classes.

Example

Peyton passed *almost* three classes.

The sentence above implies that Peyton passed two, *almost* three classes. The placement of the modifier *almost* changed the meaning of the sentence.

Example

To move across the country, Sofia *just* leased a car.

The above sentence implies that Sofia did not buy or borrow a car, but leased one instead.

Example

To move across the country, Sofia leased *just* a car.

Instead of leasing a truck or a trailer, Sofia leased only a car.

▶ Misplaced Phrase Modifiers

Phrase modifiers (see Lesson 4) that describe nouns and pronouns must also be placed as closely as possible to the words they describe.

Example

A child stood next to the car who was screaming loudly.

Was the car screaming loudly? Most likely it was the child who was screaming, so place the phrase modifier *who was screaming loudly* next to *a child* in the sentence.

Edited Example

A child who was screaming loudly stood next to the car.

Example

I found a bag in the ditch full of rare coins.

Was the ditch full of rare coins? If not, move the phrase modifier.

Edited Example

I found a bag full of rare coins in the ditch.

When proofreading your writing, check carefully to make sure that the modifiers give your sentences the correct meaning.

Exercise 3

Revise the following sentences to correct the misplaced modifiers. Write the corrected sentence on the lines provided. Answers can be found at the end of the lesson.

19. I ordered a sweater from a catalog for my mother that was too small.

_____

_____

20. Taisha bought a hamburger last night that was burnt.

_____

_____

21. My friends and I were told about dangerous Halloween candy by the teacher.

_____

_____

22. Maxim nearly ran the mile in four minutes flat.

_____

_____

23. I only watched the first half of the game.

_____

24. I got a cut on my finger from a fire hydrant that is bleeding.

_____

_____

▶ Dangling Modifiers

Words, phrases, and clauses that begin a sentence and are set off by commas are called _dangling modifiers_. They sometimes modify the wrong noun or pronoun. To revise dangling modifiers, add a word so that it is more clear which noun or pronoun they are modifying, or turn the phrase into a clause by giving it a subject.

Incorrect Example
Studying for the test, many facts can be learned.

   Are the facts studying for the test? Add a clear subject for the dangling modifier to modify more clearly.

Edited Example
Studying for the test, I can learn many facts.

Incorrect Example
To learn more, the school offers night classes.

   The school wants to learn more? Turn the dangling modifier into a clause by adding a subject.

Edited Example
For the students to learn more, the school offers night classes.

Exercise 4

Revise the following sentences to correct the dangling modifiers. Write the corrected sentence on the line provided. Answers can be found at the end of the lesson.

25. Reading the encyclopedia, many important facts are learned.

_____

_____

26. After agreeing to trim the hedge, the clippers could not be found.

_____

_____

27. Looking out of the window, the rain poured down.

_____

_____

28. While eating dinner, the doorbell rang.

_____

Summary

This lesson has shown you how to use modifiers correctly in your writing. When you revise your writing, be careful to use adjectives, adverbs, and phrase modifiers correctly.

▶ Answers

Exercise 1
1. easily, adverb
2. nervous, adjective
3. quickly, adverb
4. prominently, adverb
5. loudly, adverb
6. bad, adjective
7. shyly, adverb
8. sadly, adverb

Exercise 2
9. well, adverb
10. fewer, adjective
11. bad, adjective
12. those, adjective
13. slowly, adverb
14. good, adjective
15. badly, adverb
16. fewer, adjective
17. really, adverb
18. those, adjective

Exercise 3
19. A sweater that I ordered for my mother from a catalog was too small.
20. Last night Taisha bought a hamburger that was burnt.
21. My friends and I were told by the teacher about dangerous Halloween candy.
22. Maxim ran the mile in nearly four minutes flat.
23. I watched only the first half of the game.
24. I got a cut that is bleeding on my finger from a fire hydrant.

Exercise 4
25. Reading the encyclopedia, I can learn many important facts.
26. After I agreed to trim the hedge, I could not find the clippers.
27. While I looked out of the window, the rain poured down.
28. While we were eating dinner, the doorbell rang.

12 ▶ Checking Capitalization and Spelling

LESSON SUMMARY

Capitalization and spelling are two of the most important parts of your writing. The first half of this lesson discusses which words to capitalize in a sentence, including proper nouns and adjectives. The second half offers general spelling rules and a list of commonly misspelled words. To proofread your writing expertly, it is good to have knowledge of these fundamentals.

ollowing are some general rules that can be applied to almost any situation in your writing.

- *First Words*

  Capitalize the first word of a sentence. If the first word is a number, write it as a word.

Example

Thirty-five soldiers lined up in front of the barracks.

- *I, B.C.E., A.D.*

  Capitalize the pronoun *I*, including when it is used in the contraction *I'm*. The abbreviations *B.C.E.* and *A.D.* appear as small caps.

■ *Quotation*

Capitalize the first word of a direct quotation. A direct quotation contains a person's exact words, whether they were spoken or written.

Example

Theodore Roosevelt said, "Speak softly and carry a big stick."

■ Do not capitalize the first word of a quoted sentence fragment.

Example

I agree with Theodore Roosevelt when he said to "carry a big stick."

■ *Poetry*

Traditionally in poetry, the first word in each line is capitalized, although poetry is a form of writing that commonly breaks the rules of grammar. Many contemporary poets do not always use the traditional forms. Very often you will read poetry in which the first lines are not capitalized, and sometimes there are no capitalized words in the entire poem.

▶ Exercise 1

Select the letter for the correctly capitalized sentence. Answers can be found at the end of the lesson.

1. a. my coffee was cold, so I asked the waiter to bring me a fresh cup.
b. My coffee was cold, so I asked the waiter to bring me a fresh cup.
c. My coffee was cold, so i asked the waiter to bring me a fresh cup.

2. a. We studied cave paintings dated some time before 600 b.c.e.
b. we studied cave paintings dated some time before 600 B.C.E.
c. We studied cave paintings dated some time before 600 B.C.E.

3. a. Shirley said, "My cactus has been over-watered!"
b. Shirley said, "my cactus has been over-watered!"
c. shirley said, "My cactus has been over-watered!"

4. a. I have never heard of a plant being "Over-watered."
b. i have never heard of a plant being "Over-watered."
c. I have never heard of a plant being "over-watered."

▶ Proper Nouns and Proper Adjectives

All nouns and adjectives that name a specific person, place, or thing must be capitalized. These are called *proper nouns* and *proper adjectives*. You must know which words to capitalize in order to successfully proofread, edit, and revise your paper.

Names of People
Examples

Doug Forrest, Madonna, Martin Luther King, Jr., Liam McAndrew, Christine MacMurray, James McDonald, Bob O'Casey, Juan de la Cruz, Jean LaFitte, Ali ben-Ari

It is necessary to find out exactly how to spell and capitalize names, as the custom varies. It is important to get names right as a sign of respect and because incorrect capitalization of a name could indicate a different person.

Family Members

Examples
Uncle Jeff, Aunt Sharon, Cousin Heidi, Grandma, Grandpa, Dad, Mom, my cousin Karl

When a possessive like *my* comes first, do not capitalize the relationship word.

Example
my dad

Brand Names of Products

Examples
Boar's Head® ham, Band-Aid®, Kleenex®, Volkswagen® Jetta

Official Titles

Examples
Mayor Jefferson, Governor Davis, Justice O'Connor, President Carter, Superintendent Levy, Dean Ross, Prime Minister Sulla, Secretary General Annan, Queen Elizabeth

Capitalize the title only when followed by a name. If the person is a high government official or someone to whom you wish to show respect, you may capitalize the title when it is not followed by a name.

Examples
Dr. Fitzgerald, chancellor of schools; Halle Chapman, class president; the Secretary of State; the Prince of Wales

Names of Structures and Buildings

Examples
Empire State Building, Golden Gate Bridge, Space Needle, Veteran's Stadium

Do not capitalize the unimportant words of the name of a structure or building.

Examples
Mall of the Americas, Bridge of the Gods, Tavern on the Green

Exercise 2

Select the letter for the correctly capitalized sentence. Answers can be found at the end of the lesson.

5. a. He made a sandwich out of wonder bread®
and oven-gold turkey.
   b. He made a sandwich out of Wonder Bread®
and Ovengold® turkey.

6. a. Uncle Fred sat next to my cousin Brenna.
   b. Uncle Fred sat next to my Cousin Brenna.

7. a. Many citizens appreciated mayor Giuliani's
presence at the many funerals.
   b. Many citizens appreciated Mayor Giuliani's
presence at the many funerals.

8. a. Her cycling trip did not cross the Bridge of
the Gods.
   b. Her cycling trip did not cross the bridge of
the Gods.

Ethnic Groups, Races, Languages, and Nationalities

Examples
Asian American, French, Latino, Japanese

Avoid capitalizing words modified by proper adjectives such as the ones above.

Examples
Mexican restaurant (unless the restaurant is named, such as Consuela's Mexican Restaurant), British beer, African music

Historical Events, Periods, Documents

Examples

Revolutionary War, Middle Ages, Bronze Age, Bill of Rights

Cities, States, and Governmental Units

Examples

Tuscaloosa, North Dakota; People's Republic of China

Capitalize the proper adjective form of cities and states, also.

Examples

Alabaman, Seattleite, Idahoan, Rhode Islander

Institutions, Organizations, and Businesses

Examples

Evergreen State College, Wesleyan University, Girl Scouts®, First Independence Bank

Exercise 3

Circle the letter for the correctly capitalized sentence. Answers can be found at the end of the lesson.

9. **a.** President Lincoln wrote the gettysburg address.
   b. President Lincoln wrote the Gettysburg Address.

10. **a.** For my birthday, we ate Chinese food and saw a movie.
    b. For my birthday, we ate chinese food and saw a movie.

11. **a.** My brother Dean attended North Seattle Community College.
    b. My brother Dean attended north seattle community college.

12. **a.** The Indianapolis 500 is a huge event for Indianans.
    b. The Indianapolis 500 is a huge event for indianans.

Days of the Week

Examples

Sunday, Monday, Tuesday

Months

Examples

June, November

Special Events and Calendar Events

Examples

Fall Harvest Festival, The Great American Smoke-out, Spring Break, Groundhog's Day, Father's Day

Holidays

Examples

Christmas, Ramadan, Yom Kippur, Kwanzaa, Chinese New Year

Exercise 4

Select the letter for the correctly capitalized sentence. Answers can be found at the end of the lesson.

13. **a.** My birthday falls on a sunday.
    b. My birthday falls on a Sunday.

14. **a.** The Fourth of July is my favorite holiday.
    b. The fourth of july is my favorite holiday.

15. **a.** My friend hopes to run in the boston marathon.
    b. My friend hopes to run in the Boston Marathon.

16. **a.** It was not as cold last February.
    b. It was not as cold last february.

Works of Art and Literature

Examples

Romeo and Juliet (play), *The Scarlet Letter* (book), *Mean Streets* (film), "Where the Sidewalk Ends" (poem), *Girl with a Pearl Earring* (painting)

Names of Trains, Ships, and Other Modes of Transportation

Examples

Discovery, Mayflower, United Airlines, Starlight Express

Streets, Highways, and Roads

Examples

Broadway, Interstate 80, Best Road, Fiftieth Avenue

Public Parks and Bodies of Water

Examples

Deception Pass, Rio Grande, Washougal National Forest, Arctic National Wildlife Reserve, Central Park

Exercise 5

Select the letter for the correctly capitalized sentence. Answers can be found at the end of the lesson.

17. **a.** Amanda sailed across the pacific ocean from Seattle to Maui.
    b. Amanda sailed across the Pacific Ocean from Seattle to Maui.

18. **a.** Jessica brought her cat home to Woodlawn Avenue.
    b. Jessica brought her cat home to Woodlawn avenue.

19. **a.** Of all of Edward Hopper's paintings, *Nighthawks* is still my favorite.
    b. Of all of Edward Hopper's paintings, *nighthawks* is still my favorite.

20. **a.** We rode a Trailways® bus to Mount Rushmore.
    b. We rode a trailways® bus to Mount Rushmore.

► To Capitalize or Not to Capitalize

Direction Words

Avoid capitalizing directions on the compass *unless* they name a specific area of the country.

Example

Several population centers are on the **East Coast**.

Example

Many African-Americans headed **n**orth to find factory work.

Seasons

Avoid capitalizing the seasons or the parts of an academic year.

Example

In the **f**all term, I hope to take Mr. Lackey's class.

School Subjects

Avoid capitalizing school subjects *unless* they name a specific course. Always capitalize English because it is the name of a language.

Example

I still have the textbook from that **h**istory course.

Example

I don't know why we have to take **B**iology I before we can do lab work.

Example

My **E**nglish class met at 1:00 in the afternoon.

Exercise 6

Select the letter for the correctly capitalized sentence. Answers can be found at the end of the lesson.

21. a. For the series with the Giants, the Braves headed west.
　　b. For the series with the Giants, the Braves headed West.

22. a. Kara needs to be excused from math class today.
　　b. Kara needs to be excused from Math class today.

23. a. I plan to go to Puerto Rico in the Summer.
　　b. I plan to go to Puerto Rico in the summer.

24. a. The Midwest had a very mild winter last year.
　　b. The midwest had a very mild winter last year.

▶ General Spelling Rules

The English language combines words from many different languages, and they do not always look the way they sound. If you know another language, such as Spanish, French, Greek, or Latin, that will help you spell in English because many English words are derived from those languages. It will also help you practice spelling correctly, just like you must practice increasing your vocabulary. When you learn a new word, concentrate not only on what it means, but how to spell it. There are also many rules to help you spell, and almost as many exceptions. Knowing the rules will help you when you write a word that you are not sure how to spell.

ie vs. ei
The Rule

When the *ie* combination sounds like long *e* (*ee*), the rule is: *i* before *e* except after *c*.

Examples
belief fierce cashier fiend wield yield
series chief achieve niece hygiene relieve

Exceptions

The *ie* combination comes after *c* when it sounds like *sh* or *sy*.

Examples
deficient conscience omniscient ancient
society science

The examples above come from the Greek root *scient*, which means knowing. *Science* means knowing.

The Rule

When the combination of *e* and *i* sounds like *ay*, the rule is: *e* before *i*.

Examples
neighbor weigh eight feint freight reign
sleigh surveillance veil vein weight skein

Exceptions

Sometimes the combination of *e* and *i* sounds like *ee*.

Examples
either weird seizure sheik leisure seize

Sometimes the combination of *e* and *i* sounds like long *i*.

Examples
height sleight stein seismology

Sometimes the combination of *e* and *i* sounds like short *e*.

Examples
their   heifer   foreign   forfeit

Exercise 7
Select the correctly spelled word in each of the following sentences. Answers can be found at the end of the lesson.

25. He did not know his exact (**hieght, height**).

26. The tape player broke, so the songs sounded (**wierd, weird**).

27. The dentist told the girls about dental (**hygeine, hygiene**).

28. I did not mean to (**deceive, decieve**) you.

▶ Vowel Combinations

The Rule
When two vowels are together, the first one is usually long and the second one is silent.

Examples
reach   cheapen   conceal   caffeine   paisley
abstain   acquaint   juice   nuisance   buoy

Exceptions
Sometimes the pair *ai* makes an *uh* sound.

Examples
Britain   porcelain   fountain   villain   curtain
certain   captain   chieftain

Sometimes you pronounce both parts of the vowel pair *ia*.

Examples
civilian   brilliant   alleviate   familiar   genial
congenial   menial   guardian

Sometimes *ia* are combined with *t* or *c* to make a *sh* sound.

Examples
artificial   glacial   beneficial   martial
commercial

▶ Silent Vowels

American English makes several vowels silent, but there is no general rule for silent vowels. For example, sometimes a silent *e* on the end of a word makes the vowel before it long, sometimes not. The best way to approach these oddly spelled words is to become familiar with them by sight.

Examples
carriage   marriage   every   chocolate
miniature   parliament   privilege   sophomore
boundary   towel   vowel   bowel

Exercise 8
Select the correctly spelled word in each of the following sentences. Answers can be found at the end of the lesson.

29. The (**captain, captian**) sounded the alarm.

30. Pleased to make your (**acquiantance, acquaintance**).

31. Jill is a (**sophomore, sophmore**) in college.

32. The hotel bathroom had a (**porcelan, porcelain**) sink.

► Consonants

In addition to silent vowels, the English language uses silent consonants. Like silent vowels, silent consonants do not follow a general rule. The best way to learn these words is by sight, just like with silent vowels.

Examples
answer autumn calm debt ghost gnarled gnaw indict kneel knight know knowledge often subtle blight pseudonym psychology rhetorical thorough through write

► Doubling Consonants

Consonants are usually doubled when adding an ending, or *suffix*, to a word.

Rule #1
When the suffix begins with a vowel (such as *–ed*, *-ing*, *-ance*, *-ence*, or *–ant*) and the word ends with one vowel and one consonant, double the last consonant.

Examples
Cut becomes *cutter* or *cutting*.
Slip becomes *slipping* or *slipped*.
Quit becomes *quitter* or *quitting*.

Rule #2
When the final consonant of the word is accented and there is only one consonant in the last syllable, double the final consonant.

Examples
Commit becomes *committing* or *committed*.
Defer becomes *deferring* or *deferred*.
Prefer becomes *preferring* or *preferred*.

Rule #3
When the suffix begins with a consonant, keep the final *n* when adding *-ness* and keep the final *l* when adding *-ly*.

Examples
Mean becomes *meanness*.
Lean becomes *leanness*.
Legal becomes *legally*.
Formal becomes *formally*.

► The Exceptions

There are only a few exceptions to the above rules. Below are just a few examples.

Examples
Draw becomes *drawing*.
Bus becomes *buses*.
Chagrin becomes *chagrined*.

► C and G

The letters *c* and *g* can be either soft or hard. A hard *c* sounds like *k*, a soft *c* sounds like *s*. A hard *g* sounds like the *g* in *girl*, a soft *g* sounds like *j*.

The Rule
The letters *c* and *g* are soft when followed by *e*, *i*, or *y*. Otherwise, they are hard.

Examples
SOFT SOUNDS
circus cycle cell circle cyclone central giant gyrate genius gipsy gymnastics gentle
HARD SOUNDS
case cousin corporate couple click crop go gab gobble glue grimy gout

The Exceptions

When a word ends in hard *c*, add a *k* before a suffix that begins in -*e*, -*i*, or -*y*.

Examples
Traffic becomes *trafficking*
Mimic becomes *mimicking*

The Exceptions to the Exception

Very few words keep the soft *c* sound when a suffix beginning with *i* is used.

plasticity   elasticity

Exercise 9

Select the correctly spelled word in each of the following sentences. Answers can be found at the end of the lesson.

33. He gave me a (**suttle, subtle**) hint about my gift.

34. Sharon was not guilty of (**commiting, committing**) the crime.

35. When the subway suddenly stopped, some people began (**panicing, panicking**).

36. The contract was (**legally, legaly**) binding.

► Final E

Rule #1

Drop the final *e* when adding a suffix that begins with a vowel, such as -*ing*, -*able*, -*ous*, or -*ity*.

Examples
Surprise becomes *surprising*.
Leave becomes *leaving*.

Desire becomes *desirable*.
Erase becomes *erasable*.
Grieve becomes *grievous*.
Desire becomes *desirous*.
Opportune becomes *opportunity*.
Scarce becomes *scarcity*.

The Exceptions

Keep the final *e* after a soft *c* or soft *g* to keep the soft sound.

Examples
Peace *becomes* peaceable.
Advantage *becomes* advantageous.
Outrage *becomes* outrageous.

Keep the final *e* when the pronunciation of the word would be changed if you dropped the *e*.

Examples
Guarantee becomes *guaranteeing*.
Snowshoe becomes *snowshoeing*.

Rule #2

Keep the final *e* before endings that begin with consonants, such as -*ment*, -*ness*, -*less*, and -*ful*.

Examples
advertisement enforcement amusement
politeness fierceness appropriateness wireless
tireless blameless disgraceful tasteful
peaceful

The Exceptions

Drop the final *e* when it comes after the letters *u* or *w*.

Examples
argue becomes *argument*
true becomes *truly*
awe becomes *awful*

▶ Final Y

When adding a suffix, a final *y* is sometimes changed to an *i*.

Rule #1
When you add a suffix to a word ending in *y*, keep the *y* if it follows a vowel.

Examples
attorneys chimneys monkeys keys stayed delayed played relayed playing relaying staying saying annoyance conveyance employable playable

The Exceptions
Examples
say becomes said
money becomes monies
day becomes daily

Rule #2
When you add a suffix to a word ending in y, change the *y* to an *i* if it follows a consonant.

Examples
Mercy becomes *merciful*.
Pity becomes *pitiful*.
Beauty becomes *beautiful*.
Busy becomes *business*.
Crazy becomes *craziness*.
Lazy becomes *laziness*.
Angry becomes *angrily*.
Busy becomes *busily*.
Healthy becomes *healthily*.
Salary becomes *salaries*.
Busy becomes *busies*.
Flurry becomes *flurries*.

The Exceptions
When you add *-ing*, keep the final *y*.

Examples
Copy becomes *copying*.
Busy becomes *busying*.
Study becomes *studying*.

▶ -able and -ible

-able Rule #1
If a root word takes the *-ation* suffix, it usually takes *-able*.

Examples
demonstration–demonstrable
imagination–imaginable
application–applicable

-able Rule #2
If a root word is a complete word by itself, it usually takes *-able*.

Examples
drink–drinkable
read–readable
search–searchable
bear–bearable

-able Rule #3
If a word ends in hard *c* or *g*, it uses the suffix *-able*.

Examples
despicable navigable applicable

-ible Rule #1
If a word ends in soft *c* or *g*, it takes *–ible*.

Example
forcible invincible legible incorrigible

-ible Rule #2

If a word ends in *–ss*, it usually takes *–ible*.

Examples
repress–repressible
access–accessible
permiss–permissible
dismiss–dismissible

-ible Rule #3

If a root word is not a whole word, it usually takes *–ible*.

Example
responsible

-ible Rule #4

If a word takes the *-ion* suffix, it usually takes *-ible*.

Examples
collection–collectible
   vision–visible
   division–divisible

Exception

Predict–prediction becomes *predictable*.

▶ -ary and -ery

The Rule

The rule is that only two common words end in *-ery*: *cemetery* and *stationery* (as in "paper and envelopes for letter-writing"). The rest take *-ary*.

Examples
stationary (as in "unmoving") dictionary
military library secretary vocabulary
solitary secondary voluntary

▶ -al and -el

The Rule

The rule here is that most words use *–al*. Unfortunately, there is no real rule. These words call for sight memorizing.

Examples of -al *words*
choral dismissal legal literal tribal
personal several neutral moral magical
lyrical festival

Examples of -el *words*
cancel model kennel jewel tunnel travel
shovel panel cruel towel channel hovel

▶ Prefixes

The Rule

Usually, when you add a prefix to a root word, the spelling of neither the root nor the prefix changes.

Examples
misinformed unprepared disillusioned
infrequent illegitimate misspelled unnerved
dissatisfied

Exercise 10

Select the correctly spelled word in each of the following sentences. Answers are provided at the end of the lesson.

37. She became the (**Secretery, Secretary**) of State.

38. The (**desirable, desireable**) parking spot is next to the entrance.

39. The lost dog looked so (**pitiful, pityful**).

40. Laura was (**responsible, responsable**) for the entire project.

Summary

Whether it is capitalization or spelling, there are rules to learn and to follow. Unfortunately, there are many exceptions to the rules. As you work to improve your writing, and continue to proofread, revise, and edit, learn to recognize the words that need capitalization and memorize the correct spellings by sight.

▶ Answers

Exercise 1
1. b.
2. c.
3. a.
4. c.

Exercise 2
5. b.
6. a.
7. b.
8. a.

Exercise 3
9. b.
10. a.
11. a.
12. a.

Exercise 4
13. b.
14. a.
15. b.
16. a.

Exercise 5
17. b.
18. a.
19. a.
20. a.

Exercise 6
21. a.
22. a.
23. b.
24. a.

Exercise 7
25. height
26. weird
27. hygiene
28. deceive

Exercise 8
29. captain
30. acquaintance
31. sophomore
32. porcelain

Exercise 9
33. subtle
34. committing
35. panicking
36. legally

Exercise 10
37. Secretary
38. desirable
39. pitiful
40. responsible

13▶ Punctuating Sentences

LESSON SUMMARY

As you fine-tune your writing, you will need to punctuate *declarative*, *imperative*, *interrogatory*, and *exclamatory* sentences with end marks such as periods, exclamation points, and question marks. The rules are provided for you in this lesson.

▶ Periods

Use a period at the end of a *declarative* sentence (a sentence that makes a statement).

Example
The coffee shop closes soon.

Example
If the weather warms up, I will mow the lawn.

Use a period at the end of an *imperative* sentence (a sentence that makes a request, gives an instruction, or states a command).

Example
Drop your time sheet in the manager's box.

Example
It is best to turn off the power strip before unplugging the computer.

Example
Make a left turn at the light.

Use a period at the end of a sentence that asks an indirect question.

Examples
Have you read the Harry Potter books? (*direct question*)

My friend asked me if I had read the Harry Potter books. (indirect question)

Examples
Did you turn in the earnings report? (*direct question*)

Our boss wanted to know if we had turned in our earnings report. (*indirect question*)

Examples
Will you help me change the tire? (*direct question*)

The man asked me to help him change the tire. (*indirect question*)

Use a period after an initial.

Example
The girl's favorite character is Junie B. Jones.

Example
E.M. Forster wrote for many years.

Example
Ned A. Garnett goes by his middle name Archibald, or Archie.

Use a period after an abbreviation, including titles such as Mr., Mrs., and Dr.

Example
The note said to call Dr. Nayel Mon. or Wed. in the evening.

Note that if the abbreviation comes at the end of the sentence, you should use only one period.
Use a period after abbreviations.

Example
This year Thanksgiving falls on Nov. 28.

Example
I take the train to the Ditmars Blvd. stop.

Example
I will return to my 6 ft. by 10 ft. dorm room in Jan.

Example
Mrs. Feretovic told Oscar to be ready at 6 P.M.

Note that if the abbreviation is followed by a comma, you should use both a period and a comma.

Example
My first exam is on Thurs., and my second is the following week.

Example
My alarm clock was set for 6 P.M., so I did not wake up in time.

Exception #1

Some abbreviations have become acronyms. Acronyms are either abbreviations that are pronounced as a word, like AIDS, or widely recognized names, like FBI or NASA. They do not receive periods.

Example
Agents at the Detroit office of the CIA traced the purchase back to Canada.

Example
On Saturday, I am going to watch NASCAR with my friends.

Example
Seven Baltic states were just admitted into NATO.

In formal writing, it is best to avoid using abbreviations when possible, because they are considered informal shorthand. Titles, such as Mr., Mrs., Dr., Jr., etc., are acceptable in formal writing, as are very common abbreviations, like "P.M." Months, days of the week, and any shorthand like "b/c" for "because" should be spelled out.

The first time an acronym is used in a piece of writing, it is wise to write the name in full followed by the acronym in parentheses.

Example
The National Association for the Advancement of Colored People (NAACP) has been working toward increased civil rights for decades.

Exception #2
If an abbreviation has become a commonly used name, no period is needed.

Example
We had to go to the *auto* shop. (abbreviation for *automobile*)

Example
On the way to the *dorm,* I had to stop for *gas.* (abbreviations for *dormitory* and *gasoline*)

Example
At the *gym,* they offered free vision *exams.* (abbreviations for *gymnasium* and *examinations*)

Use a period (also known as a decimal point) before a decimal.

Example
George's grade point average was a 3.2.

Example
To simplify, we will round pi off to 3.14 when solving the next series of problems.

Use a period between dollars and cents.

Example
The portrait will cost $37.50 for the basic package.

Example
There is talk of raising the bus fare from $1.50 to $2.00 per ride.

Use a period in place of the dot when writing about the Internet. In other words, when people talk about the Internet, they say "dot," as in "dot-com." When writing about the Internet, the "dot" is a period and is not typically written as a word.

Example
We searched for information on Riddle.com.

Example
The non-profit group has a new website at Free-Billy.org that is really great.

Note that a period is not used after the Internet abbreviations that are part of the Internet address, such as *.com, .org,* or *.net.*

Exercise 1
Select the letter of the correctly written sentence. Answers can be found at the end of the lesson.

1. **a.** Dr Theodore Langley specializes in dermatology
   b. Dr. Theodore Langley specializes in dermatology.
   c. Dr. Theodore Langley specializes in dermatology

2. a. My appointment is Tues at 6:15 PM.
 b. My appointment is Tues. at 6:15 PM.
 c. My appointment is Tues. at 6:15 P.M.

3. a. My neighbor, Mrs Dougherty, had to get an M.R.I.
 b. My neighbor, Mrs. Dougherty, had to get an M.R.I..
 c. My neighbor, Mrs. Dougherty, had to get an M.R.I.

4. a. Mr. E. wanted to know if he could have his job back.
 b. Mr E. wanted to know if he could have his job back?
 c. Mr. E wanted to know if he could have his job back.

5. a. Jeanine's dorm. room is 60 sq ft.
 b. Jeanine's dorm room is 60 sq. ft.
 c. Jeanine's dorm. room is 60 sq. ft.

▶ Question Marks

Use a question mark after an *interrogatory* sentence (a word or group of words that asks a direct question).

Example
Who?

Example
All right?

Example
Has anybody seen my keys?

Remember, indirect questions are punctuated with a period as discussed above.

Sentences that begin with the 5 W's and 1 H of journalism: *Who, what, where, when, why* and *how* are usually questions.

Example
Why is everybody looking out the window?

Example
Who is that masked man?

In dialogue, *where* and *when* can also begin answers to questions. These answers are statements and are punctuated with a period.

Example
"Do you know *where* my book is?"
"*Where* you left it, probably."

Example
"When will you finish the proposal for the project?"
"*When* I get the time."

To make a statement into a question, place the subject of the sentence between the verbs of the verb phrase. In the examples below, the verb phrase is underlined.

Example
He could have played today. (*statement*)
Could he have played today? (*question*)

Example
Howard is going to the movie. (*statement*)
Is Howard going to the movie?

The verb phrase is not always separated by the subject in *interrogatory* sentences. In fact, questions can be *declarative* sentences with a question mark at the end. When read aloud, the speaker raises his or her voice at the end of the sentence to make it clear to the listener that it is a question.

Example
The lunch break has ended?

Example
It is time to go shopping?

▶ Exclamation Points

Use an exclamation point after an *exclamatory* sentence (a sentence that expresses strong feeling).

Example
I can't believe we made it!

Example
Watch out for that bus!

Use an exclamation point after an *interjection* (a word or group of words used to express surprise or other emotion).

Example
Wow!

Example
Congratulations!

Example
For Heaven's sakes!

An interjection has no grammatical relationship to the rest of the sentence. It is not a necessary part of speech, like a noun or verb.

When writing, it is best to use exclamation points only when necessary because when they are used too frequently, they lose their impact. Reading a paragraph with several exclamatory sentences is like sitting next to someone who yells in your ear. It can become annoying very quickly.

Exercise 2

Correctly punctuate and rewrite each of the following sentences on the lines provided. Answers can be found at the end of the lesson.

6. When do you think you will arrive

_____

7. Hooray The new phone books are here

_____

8. I fly from Wash, DC to San Diego, CA.

_____

9. Help The sink is overflowing

_____

10. Mr Owen heard the lecture by Howard T Sloan

_____

_____

11. On Wed I have tickets to the NASCAR event

_____

12. My sister asked if I had seen her notebook

_____

13. Cool shoes Where did you get them

_____

14. Will you check my homework for me

_____

Summary

Different kinds of sentences use different end punctuation. The most common is the period. An exclamation point adds energy, but be careful to use it selectively, so your sentences do not all have the same high energy. Question marks follow interrogatory sentences; just remember to form the sentence properly.

▶ Answers

Exercise 1

1. b.
2. c.
3. c.
4. a.
5. b.

Exercise 2

6. When do you think you will arrive?
7. Hooray! The new phone books are here!
8. I fly from Wash., DC to San Diego, CA.
9. Help! The sink is overflowing!
10. Mr. Owen heard the lecture by Howard T. Sloan.
11. On Wed. I have tickets to the NASCAR event.
12. My sister asked if I had seen her notebook.
13. Cool shoes! Where did you get them?
14. Will you check my homework for me?

14 ▶ Using Commas

LESSON SUMMARY

When you proofread your draft, it is important to mark the places where commas separate words, thoughts, phrases, clauses, dates, addresses, or items in a series.

When your readers see a comma, it indicates that they should pause before continuing to read. Commas can be overused, so it is essential to know where to place them.

▶ Introductory Words

A comma separates an introductory word from the rest of the sentence.

Example
Sadly, the summer ended.

Example
Surprised, my father spoke with a shaky voice.

Words such as *yes, no, well, why,* and *oh* are also followed by a comma when they begin a sentence. This usage is typical of the way we speak and of written dialogue. However, writers do not often use it in academic or business writing.

Example
No, I can't go to the movie.

Example
Well, I want to see the show.

▶ Introductory Clauses

Another form that is set off by a comma is the clause. Introductory clauses are always *dependent* clauses because they are not a complete sentence without the rest of the sentence.

Example
When I fell down, I twisted my ankle.

Example
Although the beach was far away, we arrived before dark.

Example
Walking to school, I stepped in a puddle.

Example
Looking at his face in the mirror, Jim saw a wrinkle.

Example
Happily surrounded by friends, Henry left the restaurant.

Note that if the two sentence parts were reversed, you no longer use a comma.

Example
I twisted my ankle when I fell down.

Example
We arrived before dark although the beach was far away.

Exercise 1
Rewrite the following sentences and add commas in the correct places. Answers can be found at the end of the lesson.

1. No I did not know that.

_____

2. Hoping for the best we drove further from the highway.

_____

3. When we visited St. Louis we saw the famous arch.

_____

4. Shocked she brought her hand up to her mouth.

_____

5. I rewound the tape, before we returned it to the store.

_____

▶ Commas with Appositives

Appositives are also set off by commas. An appositive is a noun or a pronoun that follows another noun or pronoun to identify or explain it. An *appositive phrase* is a phrase that contains an appositive.

Example
Frances, the best photographer in the state, took pictures at my wedding.

The appositive phrase *the best photographer in the state* identifies *Frances.*

Example
Ms. Vargas, the school guidance counselor, changed all my classes.

The appositive phrase *the school guidance counselor* identifies *Ms. Vargas.*

If the appositive phrase comes at the end of the sentence, there is only a comma at the beginning of the phrase.

Example
The opening act was David Grubman, a comic from Duluth.

Sometimes appositives are accidentally treated as complete sentences, but they are actually sentence fragments when left by themselves. Appositives have no verb or subject and do not express a complete thought.

Exercise 2
Rewrite the following sentences and add commas in the correct places. Answers can be found at the end of the lesson.

6. My aunt a gourmet cook prepared Thanksgiving dinner.

_____

_____

7. I took photographs of Adam Debbie's baby.

_____

_____

8. Mr. Melvin the bus driver always tells me the news.

_____

_____

9. Pretend you are King Arthur the leader of the round table.

_____

_____

10. Hasim goes bowling every Saturday an event he looks forward to all week.

_____

_____

▶ Nonessential Clauses

Clauses that are not introductory are set off by commas if they are *nonessential* clauses. A nonessential clause adds information to a sentence, but is not essential to the basic meaning of the sentence. If a nonessential clause is removed, the meaning of the sentence is not changed.

Example
Bobby's house, which is next door to mine, has a game room.

If you remove the nonessential clause *which is next door to mine*, the meaning of the sentence stays the same. The sentence is not about where Bobby's house is, but what it has in it.

Bobby's house has a game room.

Nonessential clauses usually begin with a *subordinating conjunction* such as *who, whom, whose, which,* or *that.*

If, by removing the clause, you change the meaning of the sentence, then it is an *essential* clause and is not set off by commas.

Example
All students who are failing two or more classes should be given after-school tutoring.

Remove the clause *who are failing two or more classes* and the meaning of the sentence changes.

All students should be given after-school tutoring.

This indicates that it is an essential clause and is not set off by commas.

Exercise 3

Examine the following sentences very carefully. Look for the subordinating conjunction to find the clause. If it is a nonessential clause, rewrite the sentence with commas. If it is an essential clause, write *essential* on the line. Answers can be found at the end of the chapter.

11. Randy who is one of the most talkative people I have ever met has become my friend.

_____

12. The adults who received the shot should not get the flu this winter.

_____

13. All the kittens that have had their shots are ready to be adopted.

_____

14. The letter which is strictly confidential was addressed to me.

_____

▶ Independent Clauses

An independent clause is a group of words that can stand alone as a complete sentence. Two independent clauses are sometimes joined by a conjunction such as *and, but, or, for, nor, so,* and *yet.* When two clauses are combined like this, a comma follows the first clause.

Example
I needed to buy some food, and so I went to the grocery store.

Example
Steve served well, but the volleyball team lost anyway.

Example
I locked my keys in the car, and my spare key was in my desk at home.

Exercise 4

Rewrite the following sentences and add the correct punctuation on the line provided. If the sentence is correct as it appears, write *correct* on the line. Answers can be found at the end of the chapter.

15. The computer was covered each night yet it still got dusty.

_____

_____

16. The winter storm brought eight inches of snow so all schools in the area opened late.

_____

_____

17. The glasses fell of the shelf and broke.

_____

_____

18. The Yucatan Peninsula is beautiful but it is being developed very quickly.

_____

_____

▶ Items in a Series

Commas separate items in a series to make it easier for the reader to understand. These separated items can be words, phrases, or clauses. Usually, a conjunction comes before the last item in the series. A comma is optional before the conjunction, but when you decide to use a comma in this case, you should be consistent.

Words
Example
Michelle, Jordan, Andy, and Margo went to the dance together.

Example
I made sure I had a clean shirt, shoes, jacket, and tie.

In both of the above examples, a comma separates *nouns* in a list. *Verbs* can also come in a list and be separated by commas.

Example
The lawnmower rumbled, backfired, and died.

Phrases
Example
The skateboarder spun, hopped onto the railing, slid down, and landed gracefully at the bottom of the stairs.

Example
The aliens landed their spacecraft, opened the pod doors, and stepped out into the sunlight.

Clauses
Example
Dave packed the snow gear, Melissa cleared out the trunk of the car, and Felipe made some sandwiches to eat on the trip to the mountain.

Example
The office was closed for the night, my manager was out of town, and the report had to be sent to the main office tomorrow.

Exercise 5
Rewrite the following sentences and add the correct punctuation. If the sentence is correct as it appears, write *correct* on the line. Answers can be found at the end of the lesson.

19. The water damage caused the plaster to stain crack and fall apart.

_____

_____

20. The reservations only included me Phil and Charles.

_____

_____

21. The basketball court was cracked concrete the rims were bent and the backboards were covered in graffiti.

_____

_____

22. Howard and Roberta own the jewelry store.

_____

Dates and Addresses

Put a commas between the date and the year when writing the date in a _month-day-year_ format.

Example
Walt married Jen on February 6, 1994, and then started his job with Kemper.

Example
Holly was born on April 17, 1987.

If using a _month-year_ format for the date, no comma is needed. Notice that the preposition _on_ becomes _in_ when the date is written this way.

Example
Holly was born in April 1987.

Put commas on either side of the state or province when it is used to further identify a city.

Example
Only about 1,000 people lived in Boston, Massachusetts, in the 1640s.

Example
The Liberty Bell is in Philadelphia, Pennsylvania.

Example
My favorite wax museum is in Victoria, British Columbia.

Commas separate the items in a street address.

Example
My friends found a house to rent at 1625 Pine Street N.W., Anchorage, Alaska.

Example
The job interview will take place at 3 Halsey Tower, Suite 104.

Exercise 6

Rewrite the following sentences and add commas where necessary. If the sentence is correct as it appears, write _correct_. Answers can be found at the end of the lesson.

23. The SAT exam will be administered on January 18 2004 in the school auditorium.

_____

_____

24. I sent the package to 7335 50th Street N.E. Seattle Washington 98115.

_____

_____

25. The air show was in March 1999 in Santa Clara.

_____

26. Blake left for Minneapolis Minnesota yesterday.

_____

27. The United Nations is headquartered in New York City.

_____

_____

28. The festival is in Las Vegas New Mexico in May 2004.

_____

_____

▶ Adjectives

Commas separate two or more adjectives preceding a noun.

Example
It was a cold, snowy day.

Example
I slept in a big, tall, comfortable feather bed.

Commas do not follow all the adjectives in a series. Commas are not used to separate adjectives that are thought of as part of the noun, such as *feather bed* in the example above.

To determine if a comma is necessary, place *and* between the adjectives. If the sentence still reads well, use a comma. If it is awkward or unclear, do not use a comma.

Example
The salesperson was a friendly, talkative, well-dressed man.
The salesperson was a friendly *and* talkative *and* well-dressed man.

Example
My ideal vacation destination is a warm, deserted, sandy beach with my sweetheart.
My ideal vacation destination is a warm *and* deserted *and* sandy beach with my sweetheart.

When revising sentences, changing the order of adjectives in a sentence can change whether a comma is needed. Be sure to use the test above each time you proofread.

▶ Parenthetical Expressions

Parenthetical comes from the word *parentheses*, those handy punctuation marks that separate statements used to explain or qualify a statement. In place of parentheses, you can use commas to set off such parenthetical expressions as *in fact, I believe, on the other hand, indeed, as a matter of fact, moreover, however,* and *consequently.*

Example
My bicycle, on the other hand, never uses gas.

Example
The petroleum-producing countries, consequently, began refining more oil.

▶ Contrasting Elements

When a sentence contains two ideas that contrast, separating the ideas with a comma makes it easier for the reader to understand. A conjunction such as *but* or *then* is often used, but not always.

Example
The bus arrived on time, but we were still late.

Example
The soap box derby cars ran quickly at the beginning of the race, slowly at the end.

Example
We saw the house where Diego Rivera was born, not his studio.

▶ Direct Address

Whenever the name of a person being addressed is included in a sentence, it should be set apart by commas.

Example
Do you know, Kathy, where the canned tomatoes are?

Example
Sarah, please take care of the plants while I am gone.

Occasionally, the person being addressed is not named, but identified in another way.

Example
I promise you, my friend, the tour is well worth the wait.

▶ Exclamations

Mild exclamations are also set apart by commas.

Example
Gee, the radio was turned off when we left.

Example
Man, that movie was way too long.

Exercise 7

Rewrite the following sentences and add commas where necessary. If the sentence is correct as it appears, write *correct*. Answers can be found at the end of the lesson.

29. By the end however the crowd was on their feet.

_____

_____

30. Gosh the hill looks steeper now that I am standing at the top.

_____

_____

31. You cover their point guard Norm and Hal you post up in the key.

_____

_____

32. We expected to play for an hour not ten minutes.

_____

_____

▶ Friendly Letter

Commas follow the greeting of a friendly letter.

Example
Dear Mom,

Example
Dear Jonas,

Commas also follow the closing of a friendly letter.

Example
Sincerely,

Example
Always yours,

Summary

Commas separate items and sentence elements, but they can be overused. When a reader sees a comma, he or she knows it signifies a brief pause. Revising sentences that have too many commas prevents your writing from having unnecessary pauses.

▶ Answers

Exercise 1
1. No, I did not know that.
2. Hoping for the best, we drove further from the highway.
3. When we visited St. Louis, we saw the famous arch.
4. Shocked, she brought her hand up to her mouth.
5. I rewound the tape before we returned it to the store.

Exercise 2
6. My aunt, a gourmet cook, prepared Thanksgiving dinner.
7. I took photographs of Adam, Debbie's baby.
8. Mr. Melvin, the bus driver, always tells me the news.
9. Pretend you are King Arthur, the leader of the round table.
10. Hasim goes bowling every Saturday, an event he looks forward to all week.

Exercise 3
11. Randy, who is one of the most talkative people I have ever met, has become my friend.
12. essential
13. essential
14. The letter, which is strictly confidential, was addressed to me.

Exercise 4
15. The computer was covered each night, yet it still got dusty.
16. The winter storm brought eight inches of snow, so all schools in the area opened late.
17. correct
18. The Yucatan Peninsula is beautiful, but it is being developed very quickly.

Exercise 5

The parentheses indicate the optional comma.

19. The water damage caused the plaster to stain, crack(,) and fall apart.

20. The reservations only included me, Phil(,) and Charles.

21. The basketball court was cracked concrete, the rims were bent(,) and the backboards were covered in graffiti.

22. correct

Exercise 6

23. The SAT test will be administered on January 18, 2004 in the school auditorium.

24. I sent the package to 7335 50th Street N.E., Seattle, Washington, 98115.

25. correct

26. Blake left for Minneapolis, Minnesota yesterday.

27. correct

28. The festival is in Las Vegas, New Mexico in May 2004.

Exercise 7

29. By the end, however, the crowd was on their feet.

30. Gosh, the hill looks steeper now that I am standing at the top.

31. You cover their point guard, Norm, and Hal, you post up in the key.

32. We expected to play for an hour, not ten minutes.

15 ▶ Using Semicolons and Colons

LESSON SUMMARY

Proper usage of the semicolon and colon demonstrates a thorough understanding of grammar concepts such as independent clauses and conjunctions as well as general punctuation.

Mastering the uses of a semicolon and colon will help you to edit with confidence.

▶ Semicolons between Clauses

To refresh your memory, an independent clause has a subject and a verb and can stand alone as a complete sentence. When two independent clauses about a related thought are combined into one sentence, it is a compound sentence. When a compound sentence does not contain a conjunction, such as *and* or *but*, a semicolon can be used.

Example
Gregory always donates to Toys for Tots; he feels it is important to help disadvantaged children have a happy holiday.

Example
Open the box from the top; do not use a box knife.

Example
Set down your pencils; close your test booklets.

The thoughts in the above examples are closely related, so using a semicolon makes good sense. Inserting a period after the first independent clause would cause too much of a break between ideas. When revising your writing, look for places where the conjunction can be replaced by a semicolon. Keep in mind, however, that it is ultimately a style decision and not a grammatical necessity.

▶ Semicolons and Conjunctive Adverbs

Semicolons separate independent clauses when they are joined by conjunctive adverbs.

Example
The union and management could not come to an agreement before the deadline; however, they were willing to meet again in the morning.

Example
The water level in the lower altitudes rose to unprecedented heights over the long weekend; furthermore, the base snow level rose above the tree line.

Following is a complete list of words used as conjunctive adverbs.

accordingly	furthermore	instead
otherwise	besides	hence
moreover	therefore	consequently
however	nevertheless	thus

Do not confuse conjunctive adverbs with subordinating conjunctions such as *because, though, until,* and *while.* A clause that begins with a subordinating conjunction is a subordinate clause, not an independent clause; it cannot stand alone as a sentence.

One way to determine whether a word is a conjunctive adverb is to see if it can be placed differently within a sentence. Here are two independent clauses:

The lightning storm began in the late morning. The golf game was cancelled.

There are two ways of combining these two independent clauses into one compound sentence:

The lightning storm began in the late morning; therefore, the golf game was cancelled.
The golf game was cancelled because the lightning storm began in the late morning.

The second clause in the first sentence could read, "the golf game, *therefore,* was cancelled." Since it could be placed differently, you know *therefore* is a conjunctive adverb.

In the second sentence above, try to move the conjunction *because* to a different place in the sentence. It doesn't make sense to say, "The lightning storm *because* began in the late morning" or, "The lightning storm began *because* in the late morning." In this case, *because* is clearly a subordinating conjunction, and the clause it introduces, "because the lightning storm began in the late morning," is not an independent clause.

▶ Semicolons and Phrases

In addition to conjunctive adverbs, semicolons can be used with phrases such as *for example, for instance,* and *that is.*

Example

State universities have some advantages over smaller, private colleges; for example, the variety of programs offered is typically greater at a larger school.

Example

The two coaches saw no way of resolving the issue; that is, each claimed the other was unwilling to negotiate a time and place for the make up game.

▶ Semicolons between Word Groups with Commas

If a sentence uses too many commas, the reader can become confused. Use a semicolon instead of a comma before a conjunction for the reader's clarification.

Example

Jerry will not even try Greek, Japanese, or Thai food; but he will eat anything that his mother cooks.

Example

The new bowling alley has 20 lanes, 12 video games, four pinball machines, a restaurant, and a full bar with karaoke; and the grand opening exceeded the expectations of the owners.

Use a semicolon between a series of phrases if they contain commas.

Example

The orientation for new employees will be held on Friday, October 11; Saturday, October 12; and Wednesday, October 16.

Example

The three brothers who won the lottery live in Tacoma, Washington; Minneapolis, Minnesota; and Athens, Georgia.

Exercise 1

Rewrite the following sentences adding semicolons where they are needed. Answers can be found at the end of the lesson.

1. I made it to the meeting on time however, I will drive a different route next time.

_____

_____

2. Our trip took us to New Orleans, Louisiana, Lubbock, Texas, and Nashville, Tennessee.

_____

_____

3. When taking a standardized test, read all the possible answers, do not just select the first answer that seems correct.

_____

_____

_____

4. Gordon forgot to lock the storage closet consequently, he worried that someone might use the inventory.

_____

_____

_____

5. I forgot to pack a sleeping bag, Jan, her raincoat, and Barry, his gloves.

_____

_____

6. Adam finally fixed the windows they were letting in the rain.

_____

_____

▶ Colons that Introduce

The colon is used at the end of an independent clause to introduce a list of items. The list that follows is usually an explanation of what was stated before the colon.

Example
She wanted to buy one of these cars: a Honda Accord, a Toyota Celica, or a Volkswagen Jetta.

Example
These people were selected for the business trip to Las Vegas: Joe McGarretty, Linda Anderson, and Bruce Swensen.

Do not use a colon to introduce items that complete the sentence. In other words, if the clause before the list cannot stand as a complete sentence by itself, do not use a colon.

Example
She wanted to buy a Honda Accord, a Toyota Celica, or a Volkswagen Jetta.

The clause *she wanted to buy* is not a complete thought. The list of cars answers the question *she wanted to buy what?* and therefore completes the sentence.

Example
The people selected for the business trip to Las Vegas were Joe McGarretty, Linda Anderson, and Bruce Swensen.

Colons are used to introduce a formal statement or extract.

Example
As President Theodore Roosevelt often advised: "Speak softly and carry a big stick."

Example
Leo Tolstoy, the famous author, once said: "What a strange illusion it is to suppose that beauty is goodness."

Colons are used to introduce a formal statement. Often, expressions such as *the following* or *as follows* precede the colon and no quotation marks are necessary.

Example
Mara Reilly, Chief Financial Officer, made the following observations: Communication between the many departments is vital for improving efficiency and increasing profits.

Example
When operating the One Ton Press, observe the safety procedures as follows: place the item to be pressed in the center of the plate, drop the safety guard and firmly latch it closed, and push and hold the safety button while turning the hydraulic wheel.

▶ Colons that Show a Subordinate Relationship

Use a colon to show a subordinate relationship in the following situations:

- Between two sentences when the second explains the first.

Example
Bobby hurriedly turned in the paper: He was already forty minutes late.

Example
Hilary was disappointed with her performance: She felt she could have done better.

■ Between the title and the subtitle of a book.

Example
Yesterday: A History of The Beatles

Example
Genetically Modified Foods: The Cure for Hunger or a Recipe for Disaster?

■ Between hour and minute.

Example
11:47 A.M.

Example
5:15 P.M.

■ Between volume and page number or between chapter and verse.

Example
World Book Encyclopedia IV: 113

Example
Genesis 1:2

■ After the greeting of a business letter.

Example
Dear Ms. Wallace:

Example
Vincent Mayberry, Director of Human Resources:

Note that in business letters, the closing is followed by a comma rather than a colon.

▶ Exercise 2

Rewrite the following sentences adding colons where they are needed. Answers can be found at the end of the lesson.

7. The train leaves the station at 349 P.M.

_____

8. The entire hockey team skated out onto the ice Their star forward had been hit in the face with a high stick.

_____

_____

_____

9. These employees may take their lunch at 1100 A.M. Rick Ouimet, Mercy Tullis, and Lorraine Johnson.

_____

_____

_____

10. The first line of the Gettysburg Address reads as follows Four score and seven years ago.

_____

_____

Summary

Correctly using colons and semicolons in your writing shows that you have a good understanding of clauses, phrases, conjunctions, and sentence structure. When used with accuracy, they make your writing more concise and clear.

▶ Answers

Exercise 1

1. I made it on time to the meeting; however, I will drive a different route next time.

2. Our trip took us to New Orleans, Louisiana; Lubbock, Texas; and Nashville, Tennessee.

3. When taking a standardized test, read all the possible answers; do not just select the first answer that seems correct.

4. Gordon forgot to lock the storage closet; consequently, he worried that someone might use the inventory.

5. I forgot to pack a sleeping bag; Jan, her raincoat; and Barry, his gloves.

6. Adam finally fixed the windows; they were letting in the rain.

Exercise 2

7. The train leaves the station at 3:49 P.M.

8. The entire hockey team skated out onto the ice: Their star forward had been hit in the face with a high stick.

9. These employees may take their lunch at 11:00 A.M.: Rick Ouimet, Mercy Tullis, and Lorraine Johnson.

10. The first line of the Gettysburg Address reads as follows: "Four score and seven years ago. . . ."

16▶

Using Apostrophes in Plurals and Possessives

LESSON SUMMARY

Apostrophes serve one main purpose in the English language. They show possession. They also replace letters in contractions and form the plural of some nouns. This lesson will teach you to use apostrophes correctly when revising your writing.

A postrophes are used to show that one or more things belong to one or more people or things. That is called *possession*. To form the possessive case of a singular noun, add an apostrophe and an *s*.

Example
Shakema's folder

Example
Ross's car

In words of two syllables or more that end in *s*, you *may* form the possessive by adding the apostrophe without the *s*.

Example
the Torres' party

Example
the actress' costume

There is no rule that applies to all writers in all situations with singular nouns ending in *s*. If you are writing for a particular class or company, you should check to see which style guide is used. This will determine which rule to follow. Typically, the pronunciation of the word determines whether it has an apostrophe followed by an *s* or an apostrophe before an *s*. In other words, if you pronounce it *Williamses* then punctuate it *Williams's*. If you pronounce it *Williams* as in *the Williams' garden*, then punctuate it *Williams'*.

When forming the possessive of a plural noun that ends in *s*, add only an apostrophe.

Example
the boys' basketball team

Example
the kids' various toys

Personal pronouns such as *his, hers, its, ours, yours,* and *theirs* do not require an apostrophe.

Correct Example
I believe the sandwich is *hers*.

Incorrect Example
I believe the sandwich is *her's*.

Correct Example
That game was basketball at *its* most athletic.

Incorrect Example
That game was basketball at *it's* most athletic.

Remember that these possessive personal pronouns are *not* contractions as in the incorrect example above.

Indefinite pronouns in the possessive case require an apostrophe and an *s*. Below is a list of indefinite pronouns:

another	anybody	anyone
either	everybody	everyone
neither	nobody	no one
one	other	somebody
someone		

Example
Never take another's place in line.

Example
That is somebody's hat.

Exercise 1
On the lines provided, rewrite the italicized words using the correct possessive case. If it appears in the correct form, write *correct*. Answers can be found at the end of the lesson.

1. The parking attendant misplaced *everyones'* keys.

_____

_____

2. Those are the *childrens'* books.

_____

3. The team would not refund *it's* season ticket holders.

_____

_____

4. The entire restaurant is *ours*.

_____

5. All of the *poets'* work was destroyed in the fire and she was devastated.

_____

_____

6. Mr. *Davis* social studies class went on a trip to the museum.

_____

_____

7. I left the report on my *boss'* desk.

_____

8. It is *everyone's* dream to be successful.

_____

▶ Apostrophes in Contractions

A contraction is one word made by combining two words and replacing one or more letters with an apostrophe.

Example
The contraction for *do not* is *don't*.
   Note the apostrophe replaces the *o* in *not*.

Example
For *they are* the contraction is *they're*.
   Note the apostrophe replaces the *a* in *are*.

Here is a list of common contractions:

let's   can't   shouldn't   couldn't   wouldn't
he'll   she'll   we'll   they'll   it'll   it's   what's
he's   she's   we're   they're   we've   they've
should've   could've   would've   won't

Note that the contraction *won't* combines *will* and *not*. Otherwise, when proofreading, make sure that the apostrophe is placed where the letter or letters it is replacing would have been written.

Also note that the contraction *it's* can easily be confused with the possessive *its* which has no apostrophe. One strategy for avoiding errors is to avoid contractions entirely. They are informal and can pose punctuation problems.

▶ Apostrophes to Form Plurals

When forming the plural of symbols, letters, or numbers, use an apostrophe and an *s*.

Example
When playing "tic tac toe," one player uses *x's* and the other uses *o's*.

Example
The word "unnecessary" has two *n's*.

Example
The uniform company accidentally sent two number *7's* for the same team.

When referring to words in your writing, use an apostrophe and an *s*.

Example
Run-on sentences often occur because of the overuse of *and's*.

Example

You need to clean your room with no *if's*, *and's*, or *but's*.

Exercise 2

Write the following sentences on the line provided, inserting apostrophes where they belong to make correct contractions and possessive forms. If the sentence is correct as it appears, write *correct* on the line. Answers can be found at the end of the lesson.

9. You shouldve gone to the party.

_____

10. Womens sports have become more popular.

_____

11. Do you know whats going on?

_____

12. Have you read the books on the reading list?

_____

13. Whos in charge of Rubens report?

_____

14. My cousins hat fell off at the beach.

_____

15. They can take care of themselves.

_____

16. She uses lots of *verys* in her writing.

_____

Summary

Apostrophes play an important role in making your writing clear, but they can be a source of punctuation errors. To limit apostrophe mistakes, it is important to learn the possessive forms and avoid using contractions.

▶ Answers

Exercise 1

1. The parking attendant misplaced *everyone's* keys.
2. Those are the *children's* books.
3. The team would not refund *its* season ticket holders.
4. correct
5. All of the *poet's* work was destroyed in the fire and she was devastated.
6. Mr. *Davis'* social studies class went on a trip to the museum.
7. I left the report on my *boss's* desk.
8. correct

Exercise 2

9. You should've gone to the party.
10. Women's sports have become more popular.
11. Do you know what's going on?
12. correct
13. Who's in charge of Ruben's report?
14. My cousin's hat fell off at the beach.
15. correct
16. She uses lots of *very's* in her writing.

17 ▶ Using Quotation Marks

LESSON SUMMARY

Quotation marks are used when quoting someone's exact words, when writing dialogue, when punctuating the titles of magazines and parts of books, and when setting apart words that are unusual in standard English. To add to the confusion, there are single and double quotation marks. This lesson will teach you how to apply quotation marks in your writing.

▶ Direct Quotations

Direct quotations are someone's exact words. Use quotation marks to set apart a direct quotation.

Example
The assistant manager said I am a "very quick learner."

Example
I remember him saying, "We always have meatballs on Thursday."

Example
"Who left the storage closet unlocked?" I asked myself.

Words written in print or on signs receive quotation marks.

Example

The sign at the laundromat read, "Use tables for folding clean laundry only."

Example

The website advertised, "Free shipping on orders over $100."

In academic writing, famous people are often quoted. Because these quotes are well known, it is doubly important to ensure that the quote is written exactly as it was originally said.

Incorrect Example

As Franklin Delano Roosevelt once said, "The only thing we need to fear is fear."

Corrected Example

As Franklin Delano Roosevelt once said, "The only thing we have to fear is fear itself."

▶ Dialogue

Dialogue is a form of direct quotation because you are writing someone's exact words. Dialogue is a conversation between two or more people, either real or invented, depending on whether you are writing fiction or non-fiction. Punctuating dialogue correctly involves understanding some rules beyond the rules that govern quotation marks. Dialogue requires knowledge of commas, capitalization, and end marks such as periods, exclamation points, and question marks, as well.

Example

"In the olden days, we walked two miles to school each day," said Grandpa.

The expression *said Grandpa* is known as a tag. The tag in dialogue can appear at the beginning, middle, or end of a quotation. Tags are punctuated differently depending on their placement in the sentence.

Example of tag at the beginning

Tyrone wondered, "What would happen if I used photographs from the Internet in my report?"

Note that the tag is followed by a comma, and the first word in the quotation marks is capitalized.

Example of tag in the middle of a sentence

"If I win the match," thought Beatrice, "they will have to win three in a row to be champions."

Note that a comma follows the last word in the first part of the quote and is placed inside the quotation marks. The tag is followed by a comma, and the second part of the quote is not capitalized.

Example of tag in the middle of two complete sentences

"Throughout history, there have been only a handful of leaders who came to power only in time to finish what their predecessor had begun," stated Florence. "Our President Harry S. Truman was one of them."

Note that a comma follows the last word in the first part of the quote and is placed before the quotation marks. However, when the first part of the quote is a complete sentence, a period follows the tag. Quotation marks start and end the second part of the quote, and it is capitalized.

Example of tag at the end

"Yesterday was a long time ago," remarked Bonnie's mother.

The above quotation is a sentence that would normally be punctuated with a period. Instead, a comma followed by quotation marks is used. A period is used after the tag.

Example of tag at the end with question mark
"How often does this train run?" wondered Jorge.

Note the question mark appears inside the quotation marks, but the tag is not capitalized.

Example of tag at the end with exclamation point
"Clear the way!" shouted Jan.

Note the exclamation point appears inside the quotation marks, but, as with question marks, the tag is not capitalized.

If the quote itself is not a question or an exclamation, but is included in a sentence that is a question or exclamation, the punctuation is placed after the quotation marks.

Example
Does anyone know who said, "Speak softly and carry a big stick"?

Note that the tag is a question, and the quotation is part of that question. However, the quotation itself is not a question, so the question mark follows the quotation marks. *No more than one comma or end mark is ever used at the end of a quotation.*

Each time there is a new speaker in the dialogue, begin a new paragraph by indenting.

Example
"Have you fed the cat today?" asked Miriam. "Yesterday, when I came home from work, she would not stop meowing until I gave her some food."

"I haven't fed her yet," replied Alistair, "but as soon as I can find the can opener, I will."

Exercise 1

Rewrite the following sentences adding the correct punctuation. Use the lines provided. Answers can be found at the end of the lesson.

1. The director of the program asked "who are the violin players"

_____

_____

2. "No trespassing" read the sign on the post.

_____

3. The professor told us to "line up according to height"

_____

_____

4. "I am positive" muttered Walter "that I left my keys here"

_____

_____

5. "Get out of the building" shouted the custodian "there is an electrical fire in the switch room"

_____

_____

6. Lincoln's Gettysburg Address begins "four score and seven years ago"

_____

_____

▶ Titles

Quotation marks are used to punctuate the titles of shorter works, or works that are parts of a larger work. When you refer to a published piece in your writing, be sure to cite your sources. This will eliminate the problem of plagiarism.

Example of a short story title
The class discussed Leslie Marmon Silko's "Tony's Story."

Example of a chapter title
Your assignment tonight is to read Chapter 12, "Civil Rights in America."

Example of the title of a poem
"The Lamb," by William Blake, reads like a prayer.

Example of the title of a song
We listened to "Strange Fruit" by Billie Holliday.

Example of the name of a T.V. show
"The Cosby Show" changed television comedy in the 1980s.

Example of the title of an article in a magazine or journal
Our homework was to read "The Maginot Line" from *Smithsonian Magazine*.

Note that with academic writing, it is important to cite your sources properly. Check with your supervisor or instructor to determine whether you are expected to use the Modern Languages Association or the American Psychological Association format. There are many popular citation guides that can help you; just be sure to follow the format exactly. When you conduct research, it is important to write down all the relevant information from your sources. (See the LearningExpress Skill Builder entitled *Research and Writing Skills* for instruction in this area.)

The titles of longer works such as novels, movies, epic poems, collections of poetry, the names of magazines or newspapers, plays, musicals, or long musical compositions are typically italicized, or underlined if they are written by hand.

▶ Unusual Words

Use quotation marks to set apart technical terms, slang words, nicknames, or any unfamiliar terms.

Example
My grandmother's recipe required a "zabaglione pan."

Example
According to the magazine, the new teen singer is both "hot" and "cool."

Example
They call him "Red" even though all his red hair fell out years ago.

Quotation marks are also used to indicate the use of irony.

Example
The "taxi" was actually a motorcycle with a poorly attached sidecar.

Example
The "magnificent roof garden" was actually two potted plants.

▶ Single Quotation Marks

Single quotation marks (') set apart a quotation within a quotation.

Example
"We all heard the boss say, 'The store will be closed on New Year's Day.'"

Example
"Has anybody read 'Do Not Go Gentle Into That Good Night' by Dylan Thomas?" asked Ms. Dwyer.

Exercise 2

Rewrite the following sentences on the lines provided using the correct punctuation. Answers can be found at the end of the lesson.

7. What do you suppose Carolyn meant when she said, I'm going to do something about this?

_____

_____

_____

8. The English teacher told the class, "Today we are going to read Jabberwocky by Lewis Carroll."

_____

_____

_____

9. The choir practiced Amazing Grace for the upcoming concert.

_____

_____

10. Because of her black hair, she was nick-named Raven.

_____

_____

11. "The coach told us to Start playing like we want to win! and then she stormed out of the locker room."

_____

_____

_____

12. The teenagers thought the old, dented van was mad wack.

_____

_____

Summary

The correct use of quotation marks can be confusing. When you are proofreading your writing, pay close attention to dialogue and other uses of quotation marks. Follow the rules you have learned in this lesson and your writing will be clear and graceful.

▶ Answers

Exercise 1

1. The director of the program asked, "Who are the violin players?"
2. "No trespassing," read the sign on the post.
3. The professor told us to "line up according to height."
4. "I am positive," muttered Walter, "that I left my keys here."
5. "Get out of the building!" shouted the custodian. "There is an electrical fire in the switch room."
6. Lincoln's Gettysburg Address begins "Four score and seven years ago."

Exercise 2

7. What do you suppose Carolyn meant when she said, "I'm going to do something about this"?
8. The English teacher told the class, "Today we are going to read 'Jabberwocky' by Lewis Carroll."
9. The choir practiced "Amazing Grace" for the upcoming concert.
10. Because of her black hair, she was nick-named "Raven."
11. "The coach told us to 'Start playing like we want to win!' and then she stormed out of the locker room."
12. The teenagers thought the old, dented van was "mad wack."

18 ▶ Using Hyphens, Dashes, and Ellipses

LESSON SUMMARY

This lesson will show you how to add punctuation marks like hyphens, dashes, and ellipses to your final draft.

Each of these less commonly used punctuation marks serves a purpose in your writing and, when used correctly, can add flair and style to an ordinary piece of writing.

▶ Hyphens

Hyphens are used to join words in order to create compound words such as compound nouns and compound adjectives. Compound words are words that combine two or more complete words to make one noun. Compound nouns can be hyphenated, written as two or more words, or written as one word. On the next page is a chart showing the different types of compound nouns.

HYPHENATED	SINGLE-WORD	MULTIPLE-WORD
brother-in-law	bedroom	parking lot
runner-up	laptop	compact disc
well-being	textbook	couch potato
editor-in-chief	boyfriend	window seat
problem-solver	storeroom	guitar pick
Merry-go-round	walkway	power of attorney
drive-in	doorbell	hat rack

When combining two nouns that work together as one and are equally important, use a hyphen. These are called *coequal* nouns.

Example
Robert Redford started his career as an actor, but is now known as an *actor-director*.

Example
Pete Best was a *player-coach* for the Seattle Sounders soccer team.

Example
Hector nominated Stephanie to be *secretary-treasurer*.

Compound nouns with the prefixes *ex-*, *self-*, *half-*, *post-*, *pro-*, *vice-* and *all-* or that end with the suffix *-elect* use a hyphen.

Example
Jimmy Carter, the *ex-president*, won the Nobel Peace Prize.

Example
Because he was always thinking of new ways to get the job done, he became known as a *self-starter*.

Example
We all agreed the idea was *half-baked*.

Example
The team met in the locker room to watch *post-game* videotapes.

Example
She was not just an *all-star* in her division, but she made the *all-state* team, also.

Example
After the election, the news started calling Mr. Gilligan the *mayor-elect*.

The prefix *great-* is also followed by a hyphen when it is used to show a family relationship.

Example
My *great-grandfather* Ray served in both world wars.

Example
We had Thanksgiving with Alice, my *great-aunt*.

Use a hyphen to link the parts of a compound noun that include a prepositional phrase.

Example

The big purple jellyfish is known as a Portuguese *man-of-war*.

Example

The graduate student must successfully complete a placement as a *teacher-in-training*.

Example

He became known as a *good-for-nothing* because he had no skills.

Example

On Halloween, we carved *jack-o'-lanterns*.

Example

The freight service is literally a *fly-by-night* operation.

Use a hyphen to join two or more words that function as a single adjective *preceding* the noun.

Example

The union was involved in *hard-nosed* negotiations with a *high-powered* representative from the Board of Directors.

Example

A *well-trained* dog, even a mixed breed like a cocker spaniel and poodle mix known as a *cock-a-poo*, can be sold for hundreds of dollars.

If the words functioning as a single adjective *follow* the noun, they are not hyphenated.

Example

A dog that is *well trained* can be sold for hundreds of dollars.

Example

The union negotiations were *hard nosed* and the representative from the Board of Directors was *high powered*.

Use a hyphen to avoid awkward spellings, such as when a compound word would place three of the same letters in a row, or a prefix would alter the pronunciation without a hyphen.

Example

The *bell-like* sound is actually made by a gong.

Example

The friends became *co-owners* of the café.

Example

He had a *pre-existing* condition that kept him from participating in the *re-enactment*.

Use a hyphen to join a single letter to a word.

Example

The architect used a *T-square* to design the *A-frame* house.

Example

I sent an *e-mail* message to my friend.

Use a hyphen to join numbers to words used as a single adjective.

Example

The football team practiced their *two-minute* drill.

Example

Records that play at 45 rpm's are also known as *seven-inch* records.

Series of number-word adjectives use a hyphen-comma combination except for the last item in the series.

Example
To make the bookshelves, we bought *two-, four-, and six-foot* lengths of clear vertical grain pine.

Example
Depending on their grade in school, the children ran the *forty-, fifty-, or 100-yard* dash.

Use a hyphen to write two-word numbers between 21 and 99 as words.

Example
Many people do not want to retire at *sixty-five.*

Example
All *forty-five* children bought their school supplies at the *ninety-nine* cent store.

Use a hyphen to join fractions written as words.

Example
Some experts say that humans use less than *two-fifths* of the brain.

Example
When a carpenter cuts trim boards to finish a house, they must measure within *one-sixteenth* of an inch.

Use a hyphen to write the time of day as words.

Example
We had a lunch reservation at *one-thirty* and a meeting with the house inspector at *four-o'clock.*

Example
The shuttle took off at exactly *one-thirty-seven.*

Use a hyphen to indicate a score.

Example
The Red Sox beat the Devil Rays *9-4.*

Use a hyphen to form ethnic designations that are being used as adjectives.

Example
We watched the World Cup soccer games on the big screen television at the *Italian-American* Federation.

Example
An *African-American* playwright named Lorraine Hansberry wrote *A Raisin in the Sun.*

Note that if these compounds are used as nouns, the hyphen should be omitted.

Example
The playwright Lorraine Hansberry was an *African American.*

Use a hyphen to separate a word between syllables at the end of a line. Divide a word between pronounceable parts only, divide words with double consonants between the consonants, and divide words with prefixes and suffixes between the prefix or suffix and the root word. Words that already contain hyphens should be divided at the hyphen.

Examples
hand-ball   com-mitment   pre-view   insati-able all-powerful

Never use a hyphen to separate a one-syllable word, or divide a word so that a single letter stands alone. Avoid dividing the last word of a paragraph and avoid dividing a number.

Examples of incorrect use of a hyphen at the end of a line
Do-g po-or immediatel-y aw-kward
sixty-five

Exercise 1

Rewrite the following sentences on the lines provided, adding hyphens where they are needed. Answers can be found at the end of the lesson.

1. Twenty six eight year old students visited the Lincoln Memorial.

   _____

   _____

2. The ex professional mountain bike racer is French Canadian.

   _____

   _____

3. A well spoken salesman told me about his great grandfather.

   _____

   _____

4. The post operation physical therapy consists of lifting eight pound weights.

   _____

   _____

5. Three fifths of the cars enter the S curves too fast.

   _____

   _____

6. The coach re examined the tapes of the game they lost 52 6.

   _____

   _____

7. The deck will have six, nine, and twelve foot sections.

   _____

   _____

8. The two pronged attack begins at exactly eight forty in the morning.

   _____

   _____

9. My know it all brother is the vice chair of the committee.

   _____

   _____

10. The all star pole vaulter is only five eight.

    _____

    _____

▶ Dashes

There are only a few correct uses of dashes. Many writers overuse dashes so that they detract from the content of the writing. Follow the rules listed and use dashes sparingly.

Note: A dash is a line the length of two hyphens when writing, or two hyphens in a row (--) when typing. Many computer word processing programs will automatically turn two hyphens into a dash when the next word is typed.

- Use a dash to connect a phrase at the beginning of a sentence to the rest of the sentence.

Example
Liberty, equality, fraternity—these words were the rallying cry during the French revolution.

Example
Dulles, LaGuardia, Los Angeles International—these were the first airports that received federal money to make improvements.

- Use a dash to insert a comment.

Example
The varsity team—including three junior varsity players—left today for the state tournament.

Example
Mary is organizing—with the help of the P.T.A.—a fundraiser to help cover the costs of the new gymnastics program.

- Use a dash to mark a sudden break in thought, usually in dialogue.

Example
Make a right turn here and it is the house on the—watch out for that bicycle rider!

Example
The result is that we have six weeks to finish the entire—wait, that might be McPherson now.

- Use dashes to indicate omitted letters or words.

Example
"Hello? —Yes, this is Barry. —No, I haven't seen her. —Yes, I will let her know. —Good bye."

- Use a dash to set apart a long explanatory statement that interrupts a thought.

Example
The movie—with all its fast-paced dialogue and special effects—did not hold the interest of the audience.

Example
There was a sense of doom—a sense that everything they had been working for had become worthless within the blink of an eye—when the rival company unveiled their new model.

- Use a dash after a series of items to set apart a summarizing statement.

Example
Glass, tin, aluminum, plastic, and paper—all are included in the city's new recycling program.

Example
The danceable rhythm tracks, the many guest vocalists, the amazing production—these are the reasons why this release has held the number one spot for so long.

Exercise 2

Rewrite the following sentences on the lines, adding dashes where they are needed. Answers can be found at the end of the lesson.

11. I remember where I was what Beatles fan doesn't when I heard that John Lennon was shot.

_____

_____

12. Hello? Who? I am sorry, you have the wrong number.

_____

_____

13. Speed, a strong arm, a good bat these are the tools every center fielder should possess.

_____

_____

14. The bus ride the long, boring, bumpy bus ride took twice as long as they said it would.

_____

_____

15. Thanks for the delivery and here's your wait, there's no pepperoni on this pizza!

_____

_____

▶ Ellipses

Ellipses consist of three periods in a row, but they do not serve the same function as periods. Ellipses are not end marks. Instead, they indicate material that has been omitted or long pauses, especially in dialogue.

In quotations, use ellipses to show where words have been omitted. Ellipses can be used in the middle of a quote to shorten it, or at the end of a partial quote to indicate that it continues. If the ellipses come at the end of a sentence, use a fourth period to serve as an end mark.

Example
As Nelson Mandela said, "During my lifetime I have dedicated myself to this struggle of the African people . . . it is an ideal for which I am prepared to die."

Example
"What we are learning around the world is that if women are healthy and educated, their families will flourish. . . ."

Use ellipses to indicate a pause or hesitation.

Example
The train should arrive in Phoenix at . . . six-fifty P.M.

Example
And the Golden Globe goes to . . . Sebastian Jones, writer and producer for *Friends*.

Summary

This lesson has taught you how to fine-tune your writing using less common punctuation marks like hyphens, dashes, and ellipses. Use them correctly and sparingly to add flair and style to your writing.

▶ Answers

Exercise 1

1. Twenty-six eight-year-old students visited the Lincoln Memorial.
2. The ex-professional mountain bike racer is French-Canadian.
3. A well-spoken salesman told me about his great-grandfather.
4. The post-operation physical therapy consists of lifting eight-pound weights.
5. Three-fifths of the cars enter the S-curves too fast.
6. The coach re-examined the tapes of the game they lost 52-6.
7. The deck will have six-, nine-, and twelve-foot sections.
8. The two-pronged attack begins at exactly eight-forty in the morning.
9. My know-it-all brother is the vice-chair of the committee.
10. The all-star pole-vaulter is only five-eight.

Exercise 2

11. I remember where I was—what Beatles fan doesn't—when I heard that John Lennon was shot.
12. Hello?—Who?—I am sorry, you have the wrong number.
13. Speed, a strong arm, a good bat—these are the tools every center fielder should possess.
14. The bus ride—the long, boring, bumpy bus ride—took twice as long as they said it would.
15. Thanks for the delivery and here's your—wait, there's no pepperoni on this pizza!

19 ▶ Checking for Commonly Confused Words and Clichés

LESSON SUMMARY
This lesson will show you the correct way to use several commonly confused words and how to fix any clichés you may find as you edit your writing.

Using the right word or phrase can make a big difference in your piece of writing. If you use a word incorrectly, it reflects on you and your abilities. If you choose a phrase that is a cliché, it could imply to your reader that you were too lazy to think of an original word or phrase.

▶ Homophones

Homophones are words that sound alike but are spelled differently and have different meanings.

Know/No
Know is a verb meaning *to recognize* or *understand*. *No* is an adverb meaning *not so* or *not at all*. *No* is also an adjective that means *none* or *not one*.

Example
There are *no* more musical scales that you have to *know*.

New/Knew

New is an adjective meaning *fresh* or *different*. *Knew* is the past tense of the verb *know*. It means *recognized* or *understood*.

Example
We all *knew* the *new* student from the community center.

Hear/Here

Hear is a verb meaning *listen to*. *Here* is an adverb meaning *in this place* or *to this place*.

Example
I *hear* that you are coming over *here*.

By/Buy

By is a preposition used to introduce a phrase, such as *by the way* or *by the time*. *Buy* is a verb meaning *purchase*. *Buy* is also a noun meaning *bargain* or *deal*.

Examples
We drove *by* the yard sale to see if we wanted to *buy* anything.

I ordered a computer over the Internet and it was a great *buy*.

Accept/Except

Accept is a verb meaning *agree* or *receive*. *Except* is a verb meaning *omit* or *exclude*. *Except* is also a preposition meaning *excluding* or *but*.

Examples
You must *accept* the fact that students with low grades are *excepted* from extra-curricular activities.

Everybody *except* the director thought the performance went well.

Affect/Effect

Affect is a verb meaning *influence* or *pretend*. *Effect* is a verb meaning *accomplish* or *produce*. *Effect* is also a noun meaning *result*.

Examples
We hope to *affect* the voter turnout in order to *effect* a change in our government.

The child *affected* the teacher's mannerisms but did not know the *effect* it would have.

Than/Then

Than is a conjunctive word used to make a comparison, such as *rather than*. *Then* is an adverb meaning *next* or telling *when*.

Example
Then the mechanic installed a battery that was better *than* the one that came with the car.

Passed/Past

Passed is the past tense of the verb *pass*, meaning *transferred, went by* or *ahead, elapsed, finished*. *Past* is a noun that means *history*. *Past* is also an adjective meaning *former*.

Examples
As we *passed* the movie theater, I thought about all the good times in the *past*.

Because I like to swim, my father says I must have been a fish in a *past* life.

Whether/Weather

Whether is an adverb used when referring to *possibility*. *Weather* is a noun referring to the *climate* and *conditions outside*.

Example
Whether we go skiing depends on the *weather*.

Principal/Principle

Principal is a noun that refers to the *head of a school* or an *investment*. *Principal* is also an adjective that means *main, primary*, or *major*. *Principle* is a noun meaning *law, rule*, or *belief*.

Examples
The *principal* of Parkrose High School made decisions based on a set of *principles*.

The *principal* of the mutual fund earned interest, which was our *principal* objective.

Exercise 1

Circle the correct word in the parentheses below. Answers can be found at the end of the lesson.

1. I am here to (**accept, except**) the award for winning the spelling bee.

2. Julia likes mashed potatoes more (**than, then**) stuffing.

3. Please put the sofa over (**hear, here**).

4. We (**passed, past**) the drugstore on the way to the bowling alley.

5. The (**principal, principle**) reason we are here is to determine if this is the right school for our son and daughter.

▶ Confusing Contractions

As discussed in Lesson 16, contractions replace letters in certain word pairs with apostrophes. Contractions can be confusing if they have homophones, such as the examples below.

Its/It's

Its is a possessive pronoun meaning *belonging to it*. *It's* is a contraction for *it is*.

Example
It's frustrating that my dog lost *its* collar again.

Your/You're

Your is a possessive pronoun meaning *belonging to you*. *You're* is a contraction for *you are*.

Example
You're going to drive *your* car to Philadelphia.

There/Their/They're

There refers to a *place*, like *here*. *Their* is a possessive pronoun meaning *belonging to them*. *They're* is a contraction for *they are*.

Example
They're selling balloons over *there*. *Their* prices are pretty good.

▶ Confusing Verbs

Lie/Lay

Lie is a verb meaning *to rest in a horizontal position* or *in a particular place*. *Lay* is a verb meaning *to put or place*.

They are conjugated the following way:

PRESENT	PAST	PAST PARTICIPLE
lie	lay	(have) lain
lay	laid	(have) laid

Example
Lie down and I will *lay* the covers over you.

Sit/Set

Sit is a verb that has many meanings, but the primary meaning is to *rest with the legs bent and the back upright*. *Set* is a verb meaning *to place or put*.

They are conjugated the following way:

PRESENT	PAST	PAST PARTICIPLE
sit	sat	(have) sat
set	set	(have) set

Example

Helga *set* her coffee cup on the table and crossed the room to *sit* on the couch.

Rise/Raise

Rise is a verb meaning *to go to a higher position*. *Raise* is a verb meaning *to lift to a higher position*.

They are conjugated the following way:

PRESENT	PAST	PAST PARTICIPLE
rise	rose	(have) risen
raise	raised	(have) raised

Example

I *rise* in the morning and *raise* the window shade.

Exercise 2

Circle the correct word in the parentheses below. Answers can be found at the end of the lesson.

6. Is it true that (**your, you're**) going to move to Ann Arbor to go to college?

7. I am just going to (**sit, set**) on the bench and wait.

8. The falcon swooped down and caught (**its, it's**) prey.

9. Could you (**lie, lay**) the blanket on the grass for our picnic?

10. In the barn over (**there, their, they're**), we found six baby chicks looking for (**there, their, they're**) mothers..

▶ Trios

To/Too/Two

To is a preposition used to introduce a phrase, such as *to the field* or *to the bank*. *To* is also used to form the infinitive of verbs, such as *to be* or *to run*. *Too* is an adverb meaning *also* or *overly*. *Two* is an adjective, the name of the *number* between one and three.

Example

Jimmy is going *to two* stores *to* buy his school supplies, *too*.

Where/Wear/Were

Where is an adverb referring to a *place*. *Wear* is a verb meaning *to put on, tire out, or deteriorate*. *Wear* is also a noun that means *deterioration*. *Were* is a verb, the plural past tense of *to be*.

Examples

We *were* going to reupholster the chair because of the *wear* and tear.

I need to know *where* the game is so I know which jersey I should *wear*.

Through/Threw/Though

Through is a preposition meaning *from one side to the other*. *Threw* is the past tense of the verb *to throw. Though* is a conjunction meaning *even if.* *Though* is also an adverb meaning *however.*

Example
I *threw* the ball *through* the hoop, even *though* I was not a quarterback.

Quite/Quit/Quiet

Quite is an adverb meaning *completely, very,* or *entirely. Quit* is a verb meaning *stop* or *cease. Quit* is also the past tense of the verb and means *stopped* or *ceased. Quiet* is a verb that means to *soothe* or *calm. Quiet* is also a noun meaning *tranquility* or *peacefulness. Quiet* is also an adjective that means *calm* or *silent.*

Example
I was *quite* full so I *quit* eating and stepped out onto the patio for some *quiet.*

Lead/Led/Lead

Lead is a verb that means to *guide* or *direct. Lead* is also a noun that means *front position.* It rhymes with *seed. Led* is the past tense of the verb *to lead,* meaning *guided* or *directed.* It rhymes with *red. Lead* is a noun, the name of a metal. *Lead* is also an adjective describing something made out of that metal. It also rhymes with *red.*

Examples
I will *lead* the plumber into the basement to repair the *lead* pipe.

The horse took the *lead* in the race and *led* the pack the rest of the way.

Scent/Sent/Cent

Scent is a noun meaning *odor* or *smell. Sent* is the past tense of the verb *send,* meaning *dispatched* or *transmitted. Cent* is a noun meaning *one penny,* the coin worth 1/100th of a dollar.

Examples
I *sent* my little brother to the bubble gum machine with one *cent.*

The hound dog picked up the *scent* of the escaped convict.

Exercise 3

Circle the correct word in the parentheses below. Answers can be found at the end of the lesson.

11. She (**lead, led**) the way (**through, threw, though**) the woods.

12. Bill went (**to, too, two**) the front desk and asked for (**to, too, two**) extra pillows.

13. I (**scent, sent, cent**) an e-mail to my good friend.

14. (**Where, wear, were**) can I find a (**quite, quit, quiet**) place to study?

15. The (**scent, sent, cent**) (**lead, led**) the boys to the breakfast table, (**to, too, two**).

▶ One Word vs. Two Words

The following words look quite a bit alike but have different meanings, depending on whether they are one word or two words.

Maybe/May be

Maybe means *perhaps. May be* means *might be.*

Examples
The entire office *may be* moving.

Maybe we will go to the movies tonight.

Everyday/Every day

Everyday means *ordinary* or *unusual. Every day* means *each day.*

Examples

Macaroni and cheese has become an *everyday* meal around my house.

We could eat macaroni and cheese *every day.*

Already/All-ready

Already means *as early as this, previously,* or *by this time. All ready* means *completely ready* or *totally ready.*

Example

We *already* told the bus driver that we are *all ready.*

Altogether/All together

Altogether means *completely* or *entirely. All together* means *at the same time* or *simultaneously.*

Examples

Altogether, the Latin Band has 14 members.

The dragon boats must start *all together* for the race to be fair.

▶ Two Words, Please!

The following words are sometimes written as one word, but formally should be written as two words.

All right

All right means *completely fine* or *entirely good. Alright* is informal usage and should be avoided.

Example

The airplane pilot came over the loudspeaker to tell us we would be experiencing a little turbulence but that everything would be *all right.*

A lot

A lot means *very much* or *quite a bit. Alot* is a commonly misspelled version of the words *a lot. Allot* is a verb meaning to *portion out.*

Examples

We planned to have many guests and made *a lot* of food.

The waiter made sure to *allot* an equal amount of cake to each guest.

Exercise 4

Circle the correct word in the parentheses below. Answers can be found at the end of the lesson.

16. We (**already, all ready**) bought the tickets for the concert.

17. I twisted my ankle but the next morning it felt (**all right, alright**).

18. We (**may be, maybe**) late for the meeting.

19. The chorus sang (**all together, altogether**) and it sounded great.

20. I have (**a lot, alot, allot**) of blue shirts.

▶ More Confusing Words

Agree to/with

You *agree to* something, such as a plan. You *agree with* someone else, or something, i.e., chili does not *agree with* you.

Example

I *agree to* sing in the chorus, but I *agree with* you that the songs could be better.

Between/among

Between refers to the joining or separation of two people or things. *Among* refers to a group of three or more.

Example
Between you and me, it is hard to decide which is my favorite *among* apples, oranges, and peaches.

Angry at/with

You are *angry at* a thing. You are *angry with* a person.

Example
I was *angry with* her for being *angry at* her dog.

Beside/besides

Beside means *next to*. *Besides* means *in addition to*.

Examples
Gary stood *beside* the table.
  Besides flexibility, yoga requires discipline.

Borrow/lend

You *borrow from* someone. You *lend to* someone.

Example
If you let me *borrow* a sweatshirt, I can *lend* you my jacket.

Bring/take

Bring means *move toward some person or place*. *Take* means *move away from some person or place*.

Examples
Can I *bring* this lost puppy home?
  I promise I will *take* him to the doctor when he is sick.

Can/may

Can means *able to do something*. *May* is used to ask or grant permission. It also expresses the probability of something happening.

Examples
May I have a cup of coffee?

I *can* see the end of the tunnel.

Disinterested/uninterested

Disinterested means *neutral* or *unbiased by personal gain*. *Uninterested* means *having no interest*.

Examples
The referee should be *disinterested* in the outcome of the match.

Howard was *uninterested* in any of the movies showing at the theater.

Imply/infer

Speakers or writers *imply* something. Readers, listeners, or observers *infer* something on the basis of what is heard.

Examples
The poet *implied* that giraffes look like lighthouses.

Based on what you said, I can *infer* that you disagree with the main idea.

Stayed/stood

Stayed is the past tense of the verb *to stay* which means *to remain* or *reside*. *Stood* is the past tense of the verb *to stand* meaning *to be in an upright position*.

Examples
We *stayed* in the hotel for three nights.

Jordan *stood* in line while we used the restroom.

▶ Clichés

Clichés are overused, stale metaphors. They give the impression that the writer chooses to use terms that are already known rather than creating precise and unique descriptions.

Example

I was *dog tired* so I *hit the hay*. The next morning I got up *bright and early* so I wouldn't *miss the boat*.

To avoid clichés, you must think about exactly what you are trying to say and use unique, precise, and descriptive words in place of an overused phrase.

Example with cliché
Aunt Betty is *as old as the hills*.

Revised Example
Aunt Betty's face was wrinkled like a bulldog's, and when she forgot her false teeth, which was often, her face almost folded in half.

The words you choose can add so much more meaning to your writing. The description in this example allows the reader to visualize old Aunt Betty better. However, you have to be sure all the connotations of the description fit the object or person being described. If you find bulldogs unpleasant, and want to portray Aunt Betty in a positive way, you will have to use another word to describe her; for example, you could say "Aunt Betty's face was wrinkled like a soft, old blanket."

Summary

This lesson has shown you how to use several different words and phrases that are commonly confused and how to recognize clichés in order to avoid them in your own writing. Your writing should be clear, unique, and powerful if you practice what you have learned.

▶ Answers

Exercise 1
1. accept
2. than
3. here
4. passed
5. principle

Exercise 2
6. you're
7. sit
8. its
9. lay
10. there, their

Exercise 3
11. led, through
12. to, two
13. sent
14. Where, quiet
15. scent, led, too

Exercise 4
16. already
17. all right
18. may be
19. all together
20. a lot

20 ▶ Putting It All Together

LESSON SUMMARY

This lesson will show you how to put together all the information you have learned in this book to proofread, revise, and edit your own writing.

Now that you have read the chapters and completed the lessons in this book, you are ready to work on a piece of your own writing. Print out your draft, find a red pencil, and get ready to be the editor-in-charge.

Whether you wrote with an organizational plan or not, you should take a minute to identify the way your piece is put together. After looking at the overall picture, you may decide that some rearrangement is in order. Ask yourself if the piece makes sense from beginning to end. Is the piece seamless or are there breaks in the writing where you need to add a transition or two? Are there errors that need to be corrected?

Most likely, you revised some errors as you wrote, or you may have checked spelling in the dictionary. If you worked on a computer, spell- and grammar-check programs would have notified you of some of the most glaring errors, and you may have corrected them. But, this is the time to fine-tune your writing and make it perfect. All good writers go through this process.

Remember, skip lines or double-space your draft. That makes the revision process much easier. If you did not, be prepared to write in the margin, use arrows to lead to rewritten sections, or change the color of your font to indicate revisions. Look at the sample of a first draft below.

First Draft Sample

Style is one of the big gaols of a good writer. You create a piece of Writing that accomplishes all you set out to accomplish, includes no word that stray from your purpose and is logically coherent and graceful without excess, then you achieved style. Notice I said, create a piece of writing. That is because writing good with style rarely just happens it has to be worked at, crafted, rewritten, revised, and rearranged. Your first draft are like the piece of marble that sculptors have. They look it over and see how to begin, and then they start carving with large tools like a hammer or chisels. As the scuplture progresses, the sculptors use more fine and more fine tools removing smaller and smaller piecesof marble, until they reach the finnal stage, when they polish the sculpture and place it on its base for display. Marble sculpture are beautiful to look at, completely finished, and serve the purpose of portraying a subject—a person or an object—clear and gracefully. your writing should go through a similar process of close revision until the final product is also beautiful to look at, completely revesed, and serves it's purpose.

▶ Proofreading

The process of proofreading means that you will be correcting mistakes in your writing and looking for ways to improve and perfect your writing.

Working on the Computer

If you are working on the computer, making corrections and rearranging is easy. However, you should work with a *copy* of your original draft so you can compare the changes later. This will help you see the improvements. For many but not all pro-grams, to copy your draft, click "edit," then "select all." This will highlight the entire text. Then click "edit" again, then "copy." Under "file," click "new" to open a new document. Then click "edit" again, and "paste." This will copy your draft onto a new document so that you can make any changes you want without losing the original piece. This is a wise step, because it gives you a record of the changes. You may want to return to the original wording in some cases.

As you edit and revise, you can run your piece through spell- and grammar-check programs, but remember, these programs are not foolproof, and you should double check any suggestions they make. Most word processing programs have a dictionary or thesaurus for you to use; if your program does not offer this, dictionaries and thesauruses are easy enough to access online.

As you continue to revise your work, the "cut" and "paste" functions in your word processing program allow you to rearrange words, sentences, and even paragraphs. There are disadvantages to revising on the computer, however. One problem is that you may want to compare your edited work to your original copy, and the changes may be hard to spot.

If you are a writer who likes to compare and contrast, you can use a different color or font so that the differences stand out and the edits are easy to see. To do this, you need some expertise and knowledge of the functionalities of your word processing program. Check your manual for complete instruction.

Another drawback is that proofreading symbols (as discussed in Lesson 1 and in the next section of this lesson) cannot be typed in the typical word processing program, so again, you do not have a specific record of the changes that you have made. Lastly, some problems exist whenever technology is used. For example, typos or errors in punctuation can occur because of a slip of the finger on the keyboard; printer cartridges run out of ink; computers break down; and disks can be lost, misplaced, or damaged. Perhaps you worked at the library or at a friend's house and saved the document on a computer or a disk that you now cannot access or find. Of course, technology is designed to make our lives easier, but sometimes you have to have a backup plan in order to avoid some of these mishaps.

Working with a Hard Copy

The ideal situation for most writers is to proofread, edit, and revise using a hard copy that has been double-spaced and saved on the computer. A hard copy is a copy that is handwritten or typed on paper. The main disadvantage to working with a hard copy is that any revisions you make render that copy useless. You will have to enter your changes on the computer and reprint the entire paper, or type up your paper after you have finished editing. Granted, this means additional work for you, but it is well worth the effort when you see a clean finished product.

The advantage to working with a hard copy means that you get to use some of the tools of an editor: proofreading symbols, pencils and erasers, highlighter pens, different colored inks, and correction fluid. For the rest of this chapter, it is assumed that you will be working with a hard copy.

Proofreading Symbols

Proofreading symbols (see Appendix A) make the revision process more efficient. Rather than writing a note to yourself each time you need to make a change, the symbols allow you to make a single mark. Use a different colored ink to make the symbols stand out from the rest of the text just like a teacher would do when grading your paper. Also, you can use highlighter pens to draw attention to changes, and pencil erasers and correction fluid allow you the flexibility to change your mind as well as the text.

Look again at the first draft seen earlier in this lesson. This time, proofreader's marks have been added. If some of the symbols are unfamiliar to you, see a complete list of proofreader's marks in Appendix A.

Draft with Proofreader's Symbols

Style is one of the big *central* ~~gaols~~ goals of a good writer. *When* You create a piece of Writing that accomplishes all you set out to accomplish, includes no word*s* that stray from your purpose, *and* is logically coherent and graceful without excess, then you *have* achieved style. Notice *the phrase* ~~I said~~ create a piece of writing. That is because writing ~~good with~~ style rarely just happens. *Instead, your writing* ~~it~~ has to be worked at, crafted, rewritten, revised, and rearranged. Your first draft ~~are~~ *is* like the piece of marble that sculptors ~~have~~ *select*. They look it over and see how to begin, and then they start carving with large tools like a hammer*s* or chisels. As the sculpture progresses, the sculptors use ~~more~~ fine*r* and ~~more~~ fine*r* tools, removing smaller and smaller pieces of marble, until they reach the finnal stage, when they polish the sculpture and place it on its base for display. Marble sculpture*s* are beautiful to look at, completely finished, and serve the purpose of portraying a subject—a person or an object—clear*ly* and gracefully. your writing should go through a similar process of close revision until the final product is also beautiful to look at, completely rev*i*sed, and serves it's purpose.

First Read

The next step to revision is to read the draft all the way through. Some people prefer to ignore any errors the first time; some prefer to mark every error they find immediately. Ignoring the errors allows you to get a sense of the big picture and helps you decide whether your writing says everything you want it to say. Looking for errors during the first read can get in the way, and it will be hard to make major revisions if you are focusing on a misspelling or a grammar mistake. Some drafts, however, have too many errors to read smoothly. In that case, you may have to correct the errors and make more revisions later. Remember, reading the piece aloud—whether during a first or second read—can help you hear your mistakes.

The Big Picture

When looking at the big picture, imagine you have never read the work before. Just read it through to see that it makes sense, follows a clear train of thought, and resolves the questions and ideas that it presents. You are looking for good organization, a beginning, middle, and end, logical paragraph breaks, and a clearly stated main idea. Usually, during the first read, you are not as concerned with style questions—such as tone, voice, and word choice, or with adding details, figurative language, examples, or quotes—because the piece may still go through major revisions.

▶ Revising

With the first read, you are ensuring that you have achieved your purpose. If it is an expository piece of writing, locate the main idea and see that it is addressed throughout and resolved by the end. If it is a creative piece of writing, see that it has captured the reader's interest, has been organized in the best possible way, and has avoided clichés or other trite language that undermines your voice. If the piece is intended to persuade, it should be convincing enough to do the job. These are the big picture questions that you should address.

Inserting

If you decide that you have not achieved your purpose, consider why. Perhaps your piece does not supply enough information or description. If you need to add material to your first draft, make a mark on the draft where you want to insert text, mark it #1, and then continue in sequential order with other insertions. On a blank piece of paper, write the corresponding number next to the section you want to insert. When you begin to rewrite, you can refer to the sheet and insert the new section. Always ensure that any inserted pieces do not inter-

rupt the flow of the piece. Read it through after you make your insertions to see that the transitions are smooth and the verbs or pronouns agree.

Rearranging

After reading your work, you may discover that the content is jumpy. To remedy this, rearrange or reorder your ideas by simply drawing arrows indicating where sections should be moved. Try reading it all the way through to see if the sections that have been moved adequately improve the piece. If not, try a different order. As always, double check to be sure that any new transitions are smooth.

Content

In the early stages of your writing, you should have made sure that you picked a topic that is just broad enough to allow you to do it justice within the specified word limits. For instance, a three-page essay will never be enough space to cover a topic such as "The History of France." Likewise, you would probably find it difficult to write a thirty page essay entitled "The Phillips Head Screw." Choosing an appropriate topic can make a big difference, and it should be evident that you have made the right choice as you review your writing. But, if you feel you have somehow missed the mark, now is the time to make corrections. If your topic was too broad, there may not be enough detail to support your thesis. In this case, you must narrow your topic. Weigh the facts, details, and ideas to see if there is a section in the writing that has more substance than the rest. Build on that area, and you will have a more substantial piece of writing. It may be helpful to consult your outline to see if one aspect receives more attention than others. If so, perhaps that should be your topic.

If your topic is too narrow, you do not have enough content, the piece is too short, or vital information is omitted, you must add content. Develop a list of questions that you still have about your topic, and then insert the answers to these questions in the next draft.

Second Reader

It often helps to get a second opinion. If you know someone who would be willing to read your work, ask him or her to give you some feedback. It does not have to be someone who is familiar with the topic. In fact, someone who knows little or nothing about the topic may ask more discriminating questions. Knowing what is missing from your writing gives you the opportunity to clear up the text for any reader who does not understand.

If you have a second reader, it is a good idea to bring focus and attention to one or two aspects of the piece. That way you are more likely to get the kind of feedback you need. For example, if the piece is too short or is unclear, ask the reader to look for places where it could have more detail. If the piece is too long or hard to follow, ask your reader to identify places where it could be trimmed or streamlined to make it clearer. You do not need feedback like, "It was good," or "I liked it." Ask your reader to be specific. What was good? What did you not like? What questions do you have about the topic? What do you want to know more about? Without giving your second reader an aspect to focus on, the criticism you receive is likely to be too vague to be useful.

▶ Editing

All of the steps in the revision process—prewriting, drafting, proofreading, revising, and editing—are intended to make your piece of writing clearer and therefore, better. Editing is when you really focus on trimming the fat. Imagine you have ordered a steak at a restaurant. If it consisted of half fat, bone, and gristle, you would be unhappy. You might send it back. The same is true with your writing. Cut away anything that is not "meat" before you serve it.

Editing can be a painstaking process. Analyzing your own writing is hard because you know what you meant to say. However, if you slow down and really concentrate on the words and their meaning, you can do it. Stop after each sentence to see if it is the best sentence it could be. Consult dictionaries to ensure you have used the word correctly, or check a thesaurus for a more appropriate word and to avoid repetition. Examine each sentence to see if a word or two can be cut. Eliminate auxiliary verbs, rewrite clichés, cut out redundancies, and create sentence variety. Don't be afraid that your piece will end up to be half the length it was before. Even if it does, it will undoubtedly be better.

▶ Second Draft or Final Draft?

Once you have completely proofread, revised, and edited your first draft, it is time to implement all your changes, and read it again. Hopefully, you have done more to your piece than just correct the spelling of a few words. It should be transformed through the process of revision into a concise and powerful piece of writing. By way of evaluation, you should see real differences, which mean your writing will have real impact.

Writing gives you the opportunity to craft what you want to say. In conversation, you cannot take all the time you need to form your sentences. You cannot take back words you have already said, or change the order of ideas you expressed in an argument. With writing, all this is possible, and more.

The big question is whether your second draft is your final draft. How do you decide if it is as good as it is going to get? The answer is simple. Distance yourself. Set your draft aside for a little while so you can gain perspective. When you read it again, you will most likely be a better judge of the quality. During your second read, you will notice different strengths and weaknesses than you noticed before.

Not everyone, however, has the luxury of time. Most of us are writing under a deadline. If your second draft has to be the final draft, then proofread it one more time before turning it in, just to be sure there are no glaring errors. Look at the major points. If it is about a historical figure, make sure you are spelling the name correctly. If a word is repeated throughout, double check to make sure you are using it correctly. These kinds of obvious errors draw your reader's attention to the errors and not to what you have to say. Your writing will then have less credibility. In addition, if you are expected to discuss your writing in a public forum, find out the correct pronunciation of any names or terms you have used in the work. This attention to detail can make a big difference in how your writing is received.

If you have time to set your paper aside, do so. Then return to it after a few days. Your mind will be refreshed and your eyes and ears will do a much better job of editing. Follow the same process as before. Read it for the big picture; proofread for errors; revise and edit if necessary; and create a new draft. Many professional writers return to this process over and over again before they are satisfied. Revision is the process by which your writing is crafted, and it takes time. Many people can communicate on a basic level through writing, but the revision process is where your writing is transformed from a first draft to a final draft, a precision-crafted work of art.

▶ Title

If you have not selected a title for your piece, now is the time to do so. Select a title that is appropriate for the type of writing you have done. If it is a report for work, consider your audience and choose a professional title. If it is an essay for school, follow any guidelines that are given to you, and be as creative as you can. If it is a creative or narrative piece of writing, select a title that is not too general or too trite and that relates to the piece without giving too much away. Imaginative titles for creative pieces make even more sense after the reader has finished reading.

▶ Appearance

The final step is to make your draft look as good as you can. If you are handwriting it, write the final draft carefully in blue or black ink with reasonable margins. If are typing it on a computer, avoid cute fonts and colors. Your final draft should speak for itself. It does not need a 16-point, purple, Old English font to get noticed. Presentation is important, but nothing speaks more loudly than the content of your writing. Keep the appearance clear and streamlined, just like the writing itself.

On the next page you will find a copy of the first draft that was presented in the beginning of this lesson. It has been revised and corrected. It could be a final draft, or it could be read once more to see if other changes are needed.

Revised Copy Sample

Style is one of the central goals of a good writer. When you create a piece of writing that accomplishes all you set out to accomplish, includes no words that stray from your purpose, and is logically coherent and graceful without excess, then you have achieved style. Notice the phrase, "create a piece of writing." Style rarely just happens. Instead, your writing has to be worked at, crafted, rewritten, revised, and rearranged. Your first draft is like the piece of marble that sculptors select. They look it over and visualize how to begin, and then they start carving with large tools like hammers or chisels. As the sculpture progresses, the sculptors use finer and finer tools, removing smaller and smaller pieces of marble, until they reach the final stage, when they polish the sculpture and place it on its base for display. Marble sculptures are beautiful to look at, are completely finished, and serve the purpose of portraying a subject—a person or an object—clearly and beautifully. Your writing should go through a similar process of close revision until the final product is also beautiful to look at, completely revised, and serves its purpose.

▶ Author's Checklist

Last but not least, all good writers should use a checklist. It will remind you of some important proofreading, revising, and editing steps. As you read over your work, have your checklist handy. Keep in mind, however, that different types of writing have different requirements. The checklist on the next page is designed to be applicable to all types of writing.

Writer's Checklist

Check the boxes that you feel are evident in your writing. Make a copy of this checklist and have a second reader evaluate your writing as well.

- ❏ The introduction holds the reader's attention.
- ❏ The main idea is expressed clearly and early on in the piece.
- ❏ Each paragraph discusses only one main idea.
- ❏ Each paragraph relates to and supports the main idea.
- ❏ The main idea is well-supported throughout the piece.
- ❏ The conclusion effectively wraps up the piece of writing.
- ❏ The piece follows a logical order—chronological, spatial, comparison and contrast, or another appropriate order.
- ❏ Transitions are effectively used within sentences and between paragraphs so the piece of writing flows well.
- ❏ The paragraphs are not too short or too long.
- ❏ The language and tone are appropriate for the audience.
- ❏ The tone is consistent throughout the piece.
- ❏ The sentences vary in structure and length.
- ❏ Wordiness and redundancy have been eliminated.
- ❏ Active verbs are used whenever possible.
- ❏ Subjects and verbs agree.
- ❏ Pronouns and nouns agree.
- ❏ Capitalization and punctuation are correct.
- ❏ Spelling, especially of key words, has been double-checked.
- ❏ Clichés have been eliminated.
- ❏ The title is interesting and relevant.
- ❏ If handwritten, the piece is error-free and neatly written in blue or black ink. If typed, it is in a standard, black, 12-point font with standard margins.

► Post-Test

Now that you have worked hard to improve your proofreading, revising, and editing skills, take this post-test to see how much you have learned. After you finish the test, compare your score to your score on the pretest. If your score is significantly higher, congratulations—your hard work has paid off. If your score did not improve as much as you expected, check the answer sheet to see if you answered two or more questions from the same lesson incorrectly. If so, perhaps you should review that lesson. Remember, even if your score was high, you should keep this book handy as a reference guide to use whenever you are unsure about revision techniques.

An answer sheet is provided for you at the beginning of the post-test. You may mark your answers there, or, if you prefer, circle the correct answer right in the book. If you do not own this book, number a sheet of paper from 1–50 and write your answers there. This is not a timed test. Once you have finished, you can check your answers with the answer key at the end of this test. Every answer includes a reference to a corresponding lesson. If you answer a question incorrectly, turn to the lesson that covers that particular topic, reread the information, and then try to answer the question according to the instruction given in that lesson. Take as much time as you need, and do your best.

Post-Test

1.	ⓐ	ⓑ	ⓒ	ⓓ
2.	ⓐ	ⓑ	ⓒ	ⓓ
3.	ⓐ	ⓑ	ⓒ	ⓓ
4.	ⓐ	ⓑ		
5.	ⓐ	ⓑ		
6.	ⓐ	ⓑ	ⓒ	ⓓ
7.	ⓐ	ⓑ		
8.	ⓐ	ⓑ	ⓒ	ⓓ
9.	ⓐ	ⓑ	ⓒ	ⓓ
10.	ⓐ	ⓑ	ⓒ	ⓓ
11.	ⓐ	ⓑ	ⓒ	ⓓ
12.	ⓐ	ⓑ	ⓒ	ⓓ
13.	ⓐ	ⓑ		
14.	ⓐ	ⓑ		
15.	ⓐ	ⓑ	ⓒ	ⓓ
16.	ⓐ	ⓑ	ⓒ	ⓓ
17.	ⓐ	ⓑ	ⓒ	ⓓ
18.	ⓐ	ⓑ		
19.	ⓐ	ⓑ	ⓒ	ⓓ
20.	ⓐ	ⓑ	ⓒ	ⓓ

21.	ⓐ	ⓑ	ⓒ	ⓓ
22.	ⓐ	ⓑ		
23.	ⓐ	ⓑ	ⓒ	ⓓ
24.	ⓐ	ⓑ	ⓒ	ⓓ
25.	ⓐ	ⓑ	ⓒ	ⓓ
26.	ⓐ	ⓑ	ⓒ	ⓓ
27.	ⓐ	ⓑ	ⓒ	ⓓ
28.	ⓐ	ⓑ	ⓒ	ⓓ
29.	ⓐ	ⓑ	ⓒ	ⓓ
30.	ⓐ	ⓑ	ⓒ	ⓓ
31.	ⓐ	ⓑ	ⓒ	ⓓ
32.	ⓐ	ⓑ	ⓒ	ⓓ
33.	ⓐ	ⓑ	ⓒ	ⓓ
34.	ⓐ	ⓑ		
35.	ⓐ	ⓑ		
36.	ⓐ	ⓑ	ⓒ	ⓓ
37.	ⓐ	ⓑ		
38.	ⓐ	ⓑ	ⓒ	ⓓ
39.	ⓐ	ⓑ		
40.	ⓐ	ⓑ	ⓒ	ⓓ

41.	ⓐ	ⓑ	ⓒ	ⓓ
42.	ⓐ	ⓑ	ⓒ	ⓓ
43.	ⓐ	ⓑ	ⓒ	ⓓ
44.	ⓐ	ⓑ	ⓒ	ⓓ
45.	ⓐ	ⓑ	ⓒ	ⓓ
46.	ⓐ	ⓑ	ⓒ	ⓓ
47.	ⓐ	ⓑ		
48.	ⓐ	ⓑ		
49.	ⓐ	ⓑ	ⓒ	ⓓ
50.	ⓐ	ⓑ		

1. Identify the sentence that uses capitalization correctly.
   a. Paul O'Neill and Bono toured Africa.
   b. Paul o'Neill and Bono toured Africa.
   c. Paul O'neill and Bono toured Africa.
   d. Paul O'Neill and Bono toured africa.

2. Which of the following sentences is punctuated correctly?
   a. Happily we all ate, ice cream.
   b. Happily we all ate ice cream.
   c. Happily, we all ate ice cream.
   d. Happily we, all ate ice cream.

3. Which of the following sentences is punctuated correctly?
   a. I am meeting Mr. Gordon on Tues at 9:15 A.M.
   b. I am meeting Mr Gordon on Tues. at 9:15 A.M.
   c. I am meeting Mr. Gordon on Tues at 9:15 A.M.
   d. I am meeting Mr. Gordon on Tues. at 9:15 A.M.

4. Identify the correct verb for the blank in the following sentence.
   Pete Krebs and his band _____ for their tour of Europe later today.
   a. leaves
   b. leave

5. Identify the correct pronoun for the blank in the following sentence.
   Everyone should be able to fix _____ own car.
   a. his or her
   b. their

6. Choose the best conjunction to combine this sentence pair.
   We can fly to Orlando. We can drive.
   a. and
   b. but
   c. or
   d. because

7. Identify the correct word for the blank in the following sentence.
   Irina made the job look so _____.
   a. easy
   b. easily

8. Identify the sentence that uses capitalization correctly.
   a. We went to Albany, New York to speak to governor Pataki.
   b. We went to Albany, new york to speak to governor Pataki.
   c. We went to albany, New York to speak to Governor Pataki.
   d. We went to Albany, New York to speak to Governor Pataki.

9. Which of the following sentences is a complete sentence?
   a. Tuned the guitar.
   b. Spoke at a rally.
   c. Vic cooked the rice.
   d. Because the invitation was lost.

10. Which of the following sentences is punctuated correctly?
    a. When the sun reflects off the water, it shines in my eyes, too.
    b. When the sun reflects off the water it shines in my eyes, too.
    c. When the sun reflects off the water, it shines in my eyes too.
    d. When the sun, reflects off the water, it shines in my eyes, too.

11. Which of the underlined words in the following sentence could be edited without changing the meaning?

My friend thinks love is a basic and funda mental human need.

a. my
b. thinks
c. basic and
d. human

12. Which of the following sentences uses the active voice?

a. It was suggested that we adjourn the meeting.
b. Pedro was told not to worry about making mistakes in his first draft.
c. The champagne for the anniversary party was provided by the restaurant.
d. Terry bought a very thoughtful gift.

13. Identify the correct word for the blank in the following sentence.

His hand was _____ burned.

a. bad
b. badly

14. Identify the correct contraction for the blank in the following sentence.

_____ Maria have a car?

a. Don't
b. Doesn't

15. Which of the following sentences is correctly punctuated?

a. Over the bridge. The wind is stronger.
b. The apple pie tasted good, so we each ordered a second piece.
c. The television show, starred Erik Estrada.
d. Green. My favorite color.

16. Which of the following sentences is punctuated correctly?

a. In the marina sail boats, motor boats and fishing boats are moored.
b. In the marina, sail boats, motor boats, and fishing boats, are moored.
c. In the marina, sail boats, motor boats, and fishing boats are moored.
d. In the marina sail boats, motor boats, and fishing boats, are moored.

17. The following sentence pair can be revised into one better sentence. Choose the sentence that is the best revision.

The clown is funny. The clown is in the car.

a. The clown is in the car, and the clown is funny.
b. The clown is funny and is in the car.
c. In the car, the clown there is funny.
d. The clown in the car is funny.

18. Identify the correct pronoun for the blank in the following sentence.

_____ and I ought to go home.

a. She
b. Her

19. Identify the sentence that uses capitalization correctly.

a. On Wednesday, it was my birthday, so we went to La Palapa restaurant to celebrate.
b. On wednesday, it was my birthday, so we went to La Palapa restaurant to celebrate.
c. On Wednesday, it was my birthday, so we went to La Palapa Restaurant to celebrate.
d. On Wednesday, it was my Birthday, so we went to La Palapa Restaurant to celebrate.

20. Which of the following sentences uses the passive voice?

   a. I will return the video tomorrow.

   b. It was a movie about a city girl who is adopted by a farm couple.

   c. She grows up in the country.

   d. What she learns on the farm changes her forever.

21. Which of the underlined words in the following paragraph is a transition word?

   The bicycle race takes place <u>annually</u> in California. The riders have to prepare by training in high altitudes, riding in the heat, and, <u>finally</u>, practicing together as a team. <u>If</u> they do not communicate <u>well</u> with each other, their chances of winning are slim.

   a. annually

   b. finally

   c. if

   d. well

22. Identify the correct verb for the blank in the following sentence.

   The chorus _____ during the intermission.

   a. sings

   b. sing

23. Which of the following sentences is punctuated correctly?

   a. Have you ever jumped from an airplane.

   b. Have you ever jumped from an airplane?

   c. Have you ever jumped from an airplane!

   d. Have you ever jumped, from an airplane.

24. Which of the following sentences is punctuated correctly?

   a. With the zookeepers help it's time for the tiger to have its meal.

   b. With the zookeeper's help, its time for the tiger to have its meal.

   c. With the zookeeper's help it's time for the tiger to have it's meal.

   d. With the zookeeper's help, it's time for the tiger to have its meal.

25. Circle the letter of the sentence that begins with a phrase modifier.

   a. In northern Spain, the architecture is fantastic.

   b. We made tamales all day.

   c. Am I the only person who carries a lunchbox to work?

   d. Derek drank his coffee with cream, sugar, and one cube of ice.

26. Which of the following sentences *does not* use informal language?

   a. It doesn't seem like the water tower is humongous.

   b. Later in the set, the band really started jammin'.

   c. He built the bed in woodshop class three years ago.

   d. We were hamstrung because the other members of the group were unprepared.

27. Which of the following sentences is punctuated correctly?

   a. Emiliano Zapata, a revolutionary Mexican leader, is an important historical figure.

   b. Emiliano Zapata a revolutionary Mexican leader is an important historical figure.

   c. Emiliano Zapata, a revolutionary Mexican leader is an important historical figure.

   d. Emiliano Zapata a revolutionary Mexican leader, is an important historical figure.

28. Identify the sentence that uses capitalization correctly.
   a. Our whole family will travel to Atlanta this summer to watch the U.S. nationals.
   b. Our whole family will travel to Atlanta this summer to watch the U.S. Nationals.
   c. Our whole family will travel to atlanta this summer to watch the U.S. Nationals.
   d. our whole family will travel to Atlanta this summer to watch the U.S. Nationals.

29. Identify the correct word for the blank in the following sentence.
   He is a _____ hard guy to get to know.
   a. real
   b. really

30. Identify the correct pronoun for the blank in the following sentence.
   Do you want to go to the beach with my sister and _____?
   a. I
   b. me

31. Which of the following sentences is punctuated correctly?
   a. The singer asked, "Have you heard 'To Sir, with Love' "?
   b. The singer asked "Have you heard 'To Sir, with Love'?"
   c. The singer asked, "have you heard 'To Sir, with Love'?"
   d. The singer asked, "Have you heard 'To Sir, with Love'?"

32. Which of the following sentences uses a conjunction correctly?
   a. But I want to go to the party!
   b. We played kickball I never kicked the ball.
   c. Tabitha left the flowers on the doorstep so Penny would see them.
   d. He washed the plate to put it away.

33. Which of the following sentences is punctuated correctly?
   a. The breakfast burritos in Austin, Texas can be very hot and spicy.
   b. The breakfast burritos in Austin, Texas can be very hot, and spicy.
   c. The breakfast burritos, in Austin, Texas can be very hot and spicy.
   d. The breakfast burritos in Austin, Texas, can be very hot and spicy.

34. Identify the correct word for the blank in the following sentence.
   I cannot sing very _____.
   a. good
   b. well

35. Identify the correct verb for the blank in the following sentence.
   All of the seagulls, including the brown and white one, _____ to catch the bread in the air.
   a. tries
   b. try

36. Identify the correct words for the blanks in the following sentence.
   We were _____ with the salad _____.
   a. threw, all ready
   b. threw, already
   c. through, all ready
   d. through, already

37. Identify the correct word for the blank in the following sentence.

My mechanical pencil uses very thin pencil
_____.

a. led
b. lead

38. Which of the underlined words in the following sentence is an unnecessary qualifier?

I am <u>not</u> <u>quite</u> sure if the guitar is <u>out</u> of tune <u>or</u> if it is the piano.

a. not
b. quite
c. out
d. or

39. Identify the correct word for the blank in the following sentence.

Between oil paintings or sculptures, I like sculptures _____.

a. more
b. most

40. Which of the underlined words in the following sentence is a transition word?

<u>While</u> the sun was <u>still</u> out, our group made it to the campsite; <u>meanwhile</u>, Hal's group <u>hiked</u> to the top of the ridge.

a. while
b. still
c. meanwhile
d. hiked

41. Identify the purpose of a composition with the following title:

"The History of the Internet"

a. persuasive
b. expository
c. narrative
d. descriptive

42. Circle the letter for the topic sentence in the following paragraph.

a. Even big recording stars can have difficulty with their record labels. **b.** Take Prince, for example. **c.** The story is that he changed his name to a symbol in order to get out of a bad record contract. **d.** He continues to make music today in his recording studio in Minneapolis.

43. Identify the italicized phrase in the following sentence as a participial phrase, a gerund phrase, an infinitive phrase, or an appositive phrase.

Acting like it did not matter, John sat in another seat.

a. participial phrase
b. gerund phrase
c. infinitive phrase
d. appositive phrase

44. Which of the following sentences uses the active voice?

a. Several blocks were used by the children to make the tower.
b. The children used several blocks to make the tower.
c. To make the tower, several blocks were used.
d. The tower was made using several blocks.

45. Which of the following sentences is punctuated correctly?

a. The sixty-three year old mobile uses twenty-four three-ounce weights.
b. The sixty three year old mobile uses twenty-four three-ounce weights.
c. The sixty-three year old mobile uses twenty-four three ounce weights.
d. The sixty-three-year-old mobile uses twenty-four three-ounce weights.

46. Identify the type of order used in the following paragraph: chronological order, order of importance, spatial order, or order of familiarity.

    The carnival had so many different sights to see. First, we went to the Haunted Mansion. Then, we tried to win a prize on the midway. Finally, we rode the Ferris wheel while the sun was setting. After dark, we watched the fireworks from the dock.

a. chronological order
b. order of importance
c. spatial order
d. order of familiarity

47. Identify the correct verb for the blank in the following sentence.

    Neither the dentist nor her patients ever _____ the old magazines.

a. reads
b. read

48. Identify whether the following sentence is fact or opinion.

    Sport fishing should be illegal.

a. fact
b. opinion

49. Identify the correct words for the blanks in the following sentence.

    We have our mid-winter _____ starting next _____.

a. brake, week
b. brake, weak
c. break, week
d. break, weak

50. Identify the appropriate language to use for the following situation:

    a cover letter to a prospective employer

a. formal
b. informal

▶ Answers

1. a. Lesson 12
2. c. Lesson 14
3. d. Lesson 13
4. b. Lesson 9
5. a. Lesson 10
6. c. Lesson 4
7. a. Lesson 11
8. d. Lesson 12
9. c. Lesson 2
10. a. Lesson 14
11. c. Lesson 3
12. d. Lesson 8
13. b. Lesson 11
14. b. Lesson 9
15. b. Lesson 2
16. c. Lesson 15
17. d. Lesson 4
18. a. Lesson 10
19. c. Lesson 12
20. b. Lesson 8
21. b. Lesson 6
22. a. Lesson 9
23. b. Lesson 13
24. d. Lesson 16

25. a. Lesson 4
26. c. Lesson 7
27. a. Lesson 14
28. b. Lesson 12
29. b. Lesson 11
30. b. Lesson 10
31. d. Lesson 17
32. c. Lesson 2
33. a. Lesson 14
34. b. Lesson 11
35. b. Lesson 9
36. d. Lesson 19
37. b. Lesson 12
38. b. Lesson 3
39. a. Lesson 11
40. c. Lesson 6
41. b. Lesson 7
42. a. Lesson 5
43. a. Lesson 3
44. b. Lesson 8
45. d. Lesson 18
46. a. Lesson 5
47. a. Lesson 9
48. b. Lesson 7
49. c. Lesson 19
50. a. Lesson 7

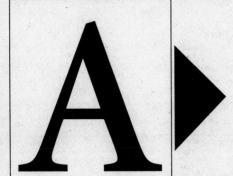

Proofreading Symbols

SYMBOL	EXAMPLE	MEANING OF SYMBOL
≡	senator Wilson	capitalize a lower case letter
/	his Uncle's house	make a capital letter lower-case
∧	just time	insert a missing word, letter, or punctuation mark
✗	desparate	change a letter
✗	over the the hill	omit a word, letter, or punctuation mark
⌒	be fore	close up space
∩	wierd	transpose letters
ⱽ ⱽ	Are you okay? he asked.	insert quotation marks
¶	¶ In the beginning . . .	start a new paragraph
⊙	set down again	insert a period
∧	so here we go.	insert a comma
(set)	When ? (set)	insert a question mark

#	bunk‖bed	insert a space
⌄∴⌄	as follows∴	insert a colon
⋏	Dubuque, Iowa⋏Lawrence, Kansas	insert a semi-colon
=	Two=tiered	insert a hyphen
⌄	Brady⌄s eagle eyes	insert an apostrophe
⌄ ⌄	"It is from ⌄Jabberwocky⌄."	insert single quote marks
—M	—M just as it should be.	insert an em dash
—N	1966—N70	insert an en dash
⁅ ⁆	⁅under the best circumstances⁆	insert parentheses
stet	Carolyn's book	(stet) let it stand
⊐	⊐with my friend Michael.	move right
⊏	⊏Turn on East Drive.	move left
⊐ ⊏	⊐Autumn⊏	center
⌐¬	Table of Contents	move up
⌊⌋	Index	move down
sp	③⑧	spell out
ital	scrupulous	set in italic type
rom	*delivery*	set in roman type
bf	in a newspaper article	set in boldface type

B ▶ Additional Resources

Proofreading, Revising, and Editing Skills Success in 20 Minutes a Day provides you with an introduction to the skills necessary to become a good writer, proofreader, and editor, but if you want to learn more, there are many ways to expand your knowledge. You can join a writing group by contacting your local community college. You can ask if they have any writing courses available or any tutors on hand who might be willing to assist you. You can also access information and classes through the Internet. Or, you can continue on your own. If you choose to do that, check this list of books. Each book listed has a short description of its contents.

▶ The Basics

It may seem obvious, but the most important reference book for you to have on hand is a dictionary. While all computers have spell- and grammar-check programs, it is always helpful to have a hard copy of a dictionary nearby. Computers can only check for the literal spelling of a word. For example, there is no way for the computer to tell the difference between the words *there*, *their*, or *they're* in a sentence. They can only verify that the word is spelled correctly. Several excellent dictionaries are:

Merriam-Webster's Collegiate Dictionary Tenth Edition
Merriam-Webster dictionaries are as complete as the *Oxford English Dictionary*. Similarly, they define words and provide examples according to standard American usage.

The Oxford American Dictionary
This dictionary, which defines words according to their American usage, is a shorter and easier dictionary to handle and use than the *Oxford English Dictionary.*

The Oxford English Dictionary
This two-volume set is also available on CD-ROM. The *Oxford English Dictionary* is the most comprehensive dictionary available in the English language. Word definitions are derived and explained from their initial origin through modern times and contemporary meaning.

▶ Other Spelling and Word Usage Gudes

These references are also handy to have around because they offer synonyms, include commonly misspelled words, and provide an easy, quick method for checking proper spelling.

The Merriam-Webster Instant Speller
This is a handy paperback book that alphabetizes frequently misspelled words. It is easy to handle and use.

Roget's International Thesaurus
Check for the most current edition. Roget's is the classic and most complete reference book for word synonyms. It also provides extensive and thorough definitions, shades of meaning, and illustrative examples.

Webster's New World Pocket Misspeller's Dictionary 2nd Edition
Check for the most current edition. This little dictionary—of over 15,000 commonly misspelled words—literally fits in your pocket. Words are arranged under easy-to-read columns labeled wrong and right.

▶ Grammar Guides and Reference Books

Again, while almost all computers have grammar checks, they often cannot answer your grammatical questions and do not provide you with examples of correct grammatical usage in context. Some essential, easy-to-use, and indispensable grammatical texts are:

Writer's Desk Reference: Ultimate Guide to Punctuation, Grammar, Writing, Spelling, Letter Writing and Much More! (New York: Scholastic, 2001)
This book provides dozens of examples for every possible grammatical question you may have. It also has a section on essay and report writing. The lively writing and excellent visual charts make this book a comprehensive companion.

Crews, Frederick and Schor, Sandra. *The Borzoi Handbook For Writers, 3rd Edition* (New York: McGraw-Hill, 1993).
This book is detailed and written for a more advanced audience. It has a complete, exhaustive, and thorough examination of all grammatical issues and provides excellent chapters on composing essays, creating paragraphs, and using grammar correctly.

Devine, Felice. *Goof-Proof Grammar* (New York: LearningExpress, 2003).
A foolproof guide to mastering the rules of grammar, this book explains the most common grammar "goof-ups" and offers simple solutions, examples, and models.

Devine, Felice. *Goof-Proof Spelling* (New York: LearningExpress, 2003).
This is a simple and easy-to-follow guide to the basic rules of spelling, which will show you how

to spot and correct common spelling errors using the simple "goof-proof" method.

Galko, Francine. *Better Writing Right Now!* (New York: Learning Express, 2002).
You will find writing strategies that work and ample opportunity to practice those strategies as your read through the lessons. This guidebook includes lots of sample essays that can help you find your writing style.

Hurford, James R. *Grammar: A Student's Guide* (Cambridge: Cambridge University Press, 1994).
Grammar is an excellent reference for all things grammatical.

Johnson, Edward D. *The Handbook of Good English* (New York: Facts on File, 1992).
This very thorough handbook covers both grammar and writing skills.

Lerner, Marcia. *Writing Smart* (New York: Random House, 2001).
With an easy-to-use format, this informative book provides instruction about general writing skills.

Olson, Judith. *Grammar Essentials, 2nd Edition* (New York: LearningExpress, 2000).
A 20-step guide to mastering the basics of grammar, this book includes interactive exercises, practical tips, and everyday examples to help you improve your written communication skills, as well as resources for continued learning.

Olson, Judith F. *Writing Skills Success in 20 Minutes a Day* (New York: Learning Express, 1998).
Opportunities to practice writing skills are offered in this book and are helpful if you want to revise your written work.

Starkey, Lauren. *Goof-Proof Business Writing* (New York: LearningExpress, 2003).
A concise, easy-to understand guide to the basics of successful business writing, this book describes the most common mistakes people make when writing at work, and offers simple rules for successful workplace communication.

Strunk Jr., William and White, E.B. *The Elements of Style, 4th Edition* (New York: MacMillan 1999).
Originally published in 1959, this slim book remains one of the best sources for good advice about editing.

Waldhorn, Arthur and Ziegler, Arthur. *English Made Simple* (New York: Doubleday, 1981).
For basic instruction in grammar, this book is a good place to start.

Williams, Joseph M. *Style: Ten Lessons in Clarity and Grace, 7th Edition* (Upper Saddle River, NJ: Pearson Education, 2002).
This writer's companion includes ten principles for writing clearly.

Summary

As you prepare to present your work to your instructor or to an audience of any kind, make sure it is error-free, clear, and interesting. Practice the proofreading, revising, and editing tips you have found in this book; use the extra resources in this section; and write a paper that you will be proud to share with others.